S0-BNQ-416

GOD'S POSITIONING SYSTEM

Following God's Plan in a Fast-Paced World

LYNETTE HAGIN

Unless otherwise indicated all Scripture quotations are taken from the *King James Version* of the Bible.

Scripture quotations marked Amplified are taken from *The Amplified® Bible.* Copyright © 1954, 1958, 1962, 1964, 1965, 1987 by The Lockman Foundation. Used by permission.

Scripture quotations marked CEV are taken from the *Contemporary English Version.* Copyright © 1995 by American Bible Society. Used by permission.

Scripture quotations marked NIV are taken from *The Holy Bible: New International Version®. NIV®.* Copyright © 1973, 1978, 1984 by International Bible Society. Used by permission of Zondervan. All rights reserved.

Scripture quotations marked NKJV are taken from the *New King James Version.* Copyright © 1982 by Thomas Nelson, Inc. Used by permission. All rights reserved.

Scripture quotations marked NLT are taken from the *Holy Bible, New Living Translation,* copyright © 1996, 2004. Used by permission of Tyndale House Publishers, Inc., Wheaton, IL 60189 USA. All rights reserved.

Scripture quotations marked TLB are taken from *The Living Bible: Paraphrased* by Kenneth Taylor. Copyright © 1971 by Tyndale House Publishers. Used by permission.

15 14 13 12 11 10 09   07 06 05 04 03 02 01

God's Positioning System: Finding God's Plan in a Fast-Paced World
ISBN 13: 978-0-89276-806-6
ISBN 10: 0-89276-806-1

Copyright © 2009 RHEMA Bible Church
AKA Kenneth Hagin Ministries, Inc.
All rights reserved.
Printed in USA

In the U.S. write:
Kenneth Hagin Ministries
P.O. Box 50126
Tulsa, OK 74150-0126
1-888-28-FAITH
www.rhema.org

In Canada write:
Kenneth Hagin Ministries
P.O. Box 335, Station D
Etobicoke (Toronto), Ontario
Canada, M9A 4X3
1-866-70-RHEMA
www.rhemacanada.org

The Faith Shield is a trademark of RHEMA Bible Church, AKA Kenneth Hagin Ministries, Inc., registered with the U.S. Patent and Trademark Office and therefore may not be duplicated.

CONTENTS

INTRODUCTION

I've always loved to travel the scenic route. I enjoy driving on the back roads instead of the main highways so I can see all the beautiful scenery. But those of us who like to travel off the beaten path sometimes need a map or GPS to help us find our way. And we need to trust the map or the instructions to keep from getting lost.

God has taken me on the scenic route many times in my life, spiritually speaking. Much as a GPS guides a traveler, God's Holy Spirit has led me past some spectacular views. He's taken me down some rough and bumpy back roads. He's guided me around some scary corners, looking down into the deep valleys. And He's also taken me along some long, winding paths. But I always knew that if I wanted to reach my divine destiny, I had to trust the Lord and not question the path on which He was leading me.

God has a path for your life too, and if you allow Him, He will direct your steps (Prov. 3:6). I've written this book to help you follow the steps He has planned for you so you can reach your dream, your divine destiny in life. You see, reaching your dream is all about paying attention—paying attention to God's instructions and not getting in a rush.

In today's fast-paced world, we are often pressured to move too quickly. But we may miss the opportunity to fulfill our dreams by always trying to take a shortcut.

1

Remember, God may not be taking you down the shorter road. He may be guiding you down the longer path. It will make all the difference in the world if you can learn how to follow your "supernatural GPS"—the Holy Spirit—and enjoy the scenery rather than complain about the ride. Then you will reach your dream—your divine destination—with joy!

CHAPTER 1

A Big Puzzle

One of the most important things in life is following God's plan, but sometimes His plan seems like a great big puzzle to us. The Lord said to me one time, "A puzzle is not a beautiful picture until you take each piece and connect the puzzle together."

Now I don't know if you've ever put a puzzle together, but when there's a lot of blue sky, trees, or water, it's so tempting to try to make a piece fit where it doesn't belong. You leave it there for a while because you think, *Oh, this has got to be the right piece. I've hunted and hunted, and I can't find another piece that fits here!* But in your heart you know it really doesn't fit.

Then suddenly, you find the puzzle piece that fits perfectly in that spot, and it makes a beautiful picture!

I believe that's the way it is with God's plan for our lives. Maybe you have only a piece or two of the puzzle in your hand right now. Or maybe several of the pieces are missing and you can't seem to figure out what the puzzle is supposed to be.

Or God may have already given you the plan for your life, and then all of a sudden He drops a piece of the puzzle into your lap that doesn't seem to fit anywhere. What do you do then?

Do you try to force that piece to fit where it doesn't really belong? Or do you put your trust in the Lord? Do you follow Him, step by step, doing what He gives you to do as He hands you one piece at a time to the puzzle of your life?

A favorite scripture of mine that always encourages me to follow God's plan is First Corinthians 2:9 (NLT)—*"No eye has seen, no ear has heard, and no mind has imagined what God has prepared . . ."* for His children.

No eye has seen, no ear has heard, and no mind has conceived the amazing things God has prepared for us. Every time I read that verse I get such an excitement in my spirit! God has many wonderful plans for our lives because He loves us and we're His precious children. But sometimes we get the pieces of the puzzle so mixed up that we can't seem to follow His plan!

No Shortcuts to the Promised Land

If you think you have trouble following God's plan for your life, imagine what it must have been like for Abraham when God first began to deal with him about going to the Promised Land. One day when Abraham was 75 years old, God told him to leave his country, the land of his fathers, and wouldn't even tell him where he was supposed to go! God said to him, "Go to a place I will show you" (Gen. 12:1).

Most of us would probably have said, "But Lord—aren't You at least going to give me a clue about where we're going?"

We would have wanted God to hand us a few more pieces to the puzzle.

But Abraham didn't question the Lord. He just loaded up all of his belongings, took his wife and family, and started out on a journey to follow God's plan.

When Abraham reached the land of Canaan, almost immediately a famine struck. If that had been most of us, we would have said, "Now, wait just a minute, Lord! This is supposed to be the Promised Land. What's happening here?"

And maybe you think that you have reached God's promised land for your life, but all of a sudden, it's famine time. Well, just hold on, because the last chapter in the book of your life hasn't been written yet!

After famine struck the land, Abraham took a wrong turn—one that led him away from God's plan. He was frightened, and his fear caused him to go the wrong way. He took his wife, Sarah, to Egypt to escape the famine, and then he told her to tell people that she was his sister. You see, Sarah was very beautiful, and Abraham was afraid the Egyptians would try to kill him if they knew she was his wife.

What a mixed-up, messed-up plan that was! And isn't that usually what happens when we try to make our own plans instead of following God's plan?

Pharaoh was so captivated by Sarah's beauty that he took her into his home, and he blessed Abraham for her sake. But the whole situation was a sin in God's sight. Pharaoh's entire household was cursed because of it, and they were struck by a terrible plague. Finally, Pharaoh found out that Sarah was Abraham's wife. He summoned Abraham and sent both of them out of the country!

Abraham Took the Leftovers

The next difficulty Abraham encountered in the Promised Land was family problems. Does that sound familiar? Fussing and fighting broke out between Abraham's family and his nephew Lot's family because there wasn't enough land for all of their cattle.

So Abraham decided to be the peacemaker. He told Lot to pick whatever part of the land he wanted for himself and his herds, and Abraham agreed to take what was left over.

Naturally, Lot chose the rich, fertile land in the Jordan River valley surrounding Sodom and Gomorrah, and Abraham took the "leftovers." Some of those rough, scraggly, rocky hillsides in the land of Canaan probably didn't look like they could support one cow, much less a whole herd of cattle. But Abraham continued to walk with the Lord, and God blessed him beyond his wildest dreams as he followed God's plan.

Mrs. Holy Ghost Leads Abraham Astray

As Abraham continued to walk out God's plan, the Lord gave him a wonderful promise. Abraham and his wife, Sarah, didn't have any children. So God told Abraham He was going to give them a child and his descendants would be as numerous as the stars in the sky (see Gen. 15:2–6). And Abraham believed what the Lord told him.

It didn't take long for Sarah to get tired of waiting for God to keep His promise. So she decided to be Mrs. Holy Ghost and try to make the promise come to pass! She led Abraham astray by urging him to have a child by one of her maidservants. What a mistake that was! He had a son, all right, and they named him Ishmael. But Ishmael brought trouble to Abraham's household.

Of course, God wasn't caught off-guard by Abraham's detour from His original plan. And the Lord had a plan to get Abraham back on track!

Later, God visited Abraham and Sarah again, and He gave Abraham a fresh word about the promise He had given him so many years before. And don't we love it when God gives us a "fresh word" about the things He's spoken to our hearts? In Abraham's case, many years had passed since God first gave him the promise to make his descendants as numerous as the stars in the sky.

When the Lord appeared to Abraham this time, He told him that Sarah was going to give birth to a child the very next year. Oh, the fulfillment of the promise was getting so close!

A little later, the Lord appeared to Abraham again and told him that Sarah would have a son. This time Sarah overheard what the Lord said to her husband, but she couldn't imagine how God could do something that wonderful. After all, she was 90 years old and she had never been able to have a child, and her husband was 100. They were the most unlikely couple in the world to have a baby! So Sarah actually laughed to herself when she heard God's promise, *and the Lord heard her laugh!*

Then God made one of the great statements in the Bible. He said, *"Is any thing too hard for the Lord?"* (Gen. 18:14). One translation says, *"I am the Lord! There is nothing too difficult for me"* (CEV).

Sure enough, it wasn't too hard for God to cause Abraham and Sarah to have a child, even in their old age. Their son, Isaac, was born the following year, and the promise of God was fulfilled!

And that tells me it's not too hard for God to fulfill His promises to you either. As you continue to follow His plan for your life, I believe you'll discover, just as Abraham and Sarah did, that nothing is too hard for our God.

A Giant Step of Faith

I can relate to the way Abraham must have felt when God spoke to him about leaving his home, the country where he had lived all of his life, and going to a strange land. You see, my husband and I experienced something like that in the early years of our marriage.

I had always known that God had a plan for my life. I had grown up in a pastor's home, and I longed to be a pastor's wife. I was very comfortable with that. But it turned out that being a pastor's wife wasn't the first thing God called me to do. Actually, it was 20 years before my husband and I began to pastor our own church.

In the meantime, I continued to follow God's plan, one step at a time. When the Lord handed me a new piece to the puzzle, I tried with all of my heart to do what He asked me to do.

But one day He handed me a really hard puzzle piece. It was something I did *not* want to do at all. The Lord asked me to do what He had asked Abraham to do—leave my own country, my own people, and go to a strange land. It was a giant step of faith for me, and I struggled with the Lord about it.

Why was it so hard for me to leave the land where I grew up? Well, I was born and raised in Dallas, Texas, the "New York of the South." Dallas is one of the fashion centers of the world, and I loved city life! But even if we didn't actually live in Dallas, I was happy as long as I lived in Texas.

Most Texans are very proud of Texas, and I was no exception. I certainly didn't want to lower my dignity and leave the land I loved, especially when my husband told me God was dealing with him about moving to Tulsa, Oklahoma! As far as I was concerned, Tulsa was just a sprawling country town compared to Dallas. Suddenly, all of my worst nightmares were coming true.

To make matters worse, God hadn't spoken directly to me about moving to Oklahoma; He had dealt with my husband. We were planning to help his father, Kenneth E. Hagin, who was traveling in the ministry at the time. But I hadn't heard from God about it at all.

I wanted to be submitted to my husband, but I also knew how important it was for me to know for myself what God was calling us to do. That way if my husband got discouraged or began to doubt what he had heard from the Lord, I could encourage him and assure him that we were obeying God.

So I began to seek the Lord, asking Him to show me whether this was His plan for our lives. As I prayed and talked to God and studied His Word, He made it clear to me that this *was* His plan for us at that time. This was the next piece of the puzzle, even though it looked like it didn't fit anywhere in what I thought was God's plan.

In June of 1972, in obedience to the Lord, my husband started working for his father as crusade director for Kenneth Hagin Ministries. The following year, we moved to Oklahoma.

Instead of preaching as he was accustomed to doing, suddenly he found himself busy with the practical details of ministry—setting up meetings, counting offerings, and making announcements. Meanwhile, I was at home, taking care of two small children and wondering what on earth God had in mind when He brought us to this place.

Our friends thought we were crazy when Ken left a position as associate pastor and we moved to Tulsa to do God-knows-what. Yes, we were crazy—crazy enough to obey the Lord.

But if we had not been willing to take that giant step of faith, even when it looked like it was wrong for us, we wouldn't be where we are today. We followed God's plan to the very best of our abilities, and He has blessed us as He promised He would in First Corinthians 2:9—beyond our wildest dreams and imaginations! And He keeps on blessing us as we do our best to follow His plan!

God's Amazing Plan

God has always had a plan for your life. He had a purpose in mind when He created you. He looked down from Heaven and said, "There's not a person on earth exactly like the person I'm about to create." And then He added, "I have a special mission for that person to accomplish."

The success of that mission depends on how we follow the plan of God for our lives. But so many times we give up on God's plan and will, and His promise for us, right before it comes to pass. So many times we do what Sarah did when she tried to make things happen in her own strength.

If we take each piece of the puzzle as God hands it to us and obey what He's telling us to do *today,* He will take care of tomorrow. And He will fulfill every word He's spoken to our hearts! Someday all the pieces of the puzzle will fall into place, and we'll see with our natural eyes the beautiful picture of God's amazing plan.

CHAPTER 2

THE BUMPS ARE
WHAT YOU CLIMB ON!

If you have decided to follow God's plan for your life, do you remember how excited you were when you first set out on the journey? But then at some point you probably found that the road wasn't always the way you desired it to be.

Sometimes there are dips and turns and even "hairpin curves" along our paths. And sometimes we find a huge pile of rocks standing in our way.

That reminds me of the story of the little boy who was leading his sister up a mountain path. The way was not easy. In fact, it was fairly rough. So the little girl said to her brother, "Why, this isn't a path at all! It's too rocky and bumpy!"

Her brother quickly replied, "But, Sister, the bumps are what you climb on!"

That's a powerful thought, isn't it? The bumps are what you climb on. There's a great deal of wisdom in that statement.

You may think, "Hey, I've had a whole lot of bumps in my life. Maybe I'm going to climb really high!" And that may be the case, because the Enemy loves to throw his biggest bumps in the paths of those who he knows are going to be great successes for God.

Will These 'Whoopsie-dos' Ever End?

Do you feel as if you've been on a bumpy ride lately? The bumps in your path may be like some of the bumps on the trails we used to ride when our family went four-wheeling. Riding a four-wheeler can be a rough experience.

On one particular trail, the way was smooth for a little while, but then, all of a sudden, it was bump, bump, bump! Those bumps were called "whoopsie-dos," because every time you went over one of them you were supposed to shout, "Whoopsie-do!"

Sometimes it felt as if my insides were literally coming apart as I skidded over the top of one of those whoopsie-dos. I was thinking, *Oh, my goodness! Will these whoopsie-dos ever end?*

And you may be saying right now, "Oh, dear Lord! Are these bumps and whoopsie-dos ever going to end?"

How did I make it through all the whoopsie-dos? There were two things that kept me going on that trail. First, I couldn't get back to camp without riding all the way to the end of the trail. And I certainly didn't want to stay out there with all of those whoopsie-dos.

Second, I knew that when I finally got past the whoopsie-dos there was going to be smooth riding. Hallelujah! I love smooth riding.

Sometimes in life we just have to take the hand of the Lord and hold on tightly and say, "Okay, God, we're going through these bumps, these whoopsie-dos, one by one, and pretty soon we're going to see smooth riding!"

Really, the attitude I've always had is this: I'm not going to allow the bumps in the road to cause me to stumble. Instead of stumbling blocks, they're going to be my stepping-stones. I'm going to step higher and higher until I climb over the top of those bumps and obstacles.

Yes, we *can* triumph over the bumps in life. I've never seen a successful person who didn't have to overcome some bumps—and even some great, big boulders and roadblocks along the way.

So if you're having mammoth trials, just know that the Enemy is trying to stop you from becoming the success God created you to be. But if you'll climb up on those bumps and use them as your stepping-stones, you can reach the top of every mountain the Lord has prepared for you.

No Foot-Dashing Stumbling Blocks

I don't know what bumps are in your path right now, but if the road before you is rocky and bumpy, I know how that feels. Thank God, there's a promise in the Bible that I go to when I feel the way is too rough. It's Psalm 91:11–12—"*For he* [God] *shall give his angels charge over thee, to keep thee in all thy ways. They shall bear thee up in their hands, LEST THOU DASH THY FOOT AGAINST A STONE.*"

Did you notice what the last part of verse 12 says—"*Lest thou dash thy foot against a stone*"? God does not promise to remove the stones and bumps from our paths. But He does promise to help us turn those bumps into stepping-stones. He promises to help us climb higher and higher on the path He's set before us, in spite of the difficulties in life.

Most of the time, we just want to complain about our troubles. Or we may try to jump over the bumps and problems or even go around them. Sometimes we get mad and try to kick the roadblocks and obstacles out of our way. What happens then? We usually find another bump or an even bigger problem staring us in the face.

Some people come to a halt when they see a bump in their path, and they refuse to go any farther. Others lose heart and turn back. But the child of God does not have to stop or go back. He can use those bumps and rocks as stepping-stones to help him climb to a higher place on the road of life.

Do you know the real problem with most of us? We're accustomed to paved roads and level sidewalks. We want everything to be smooth riding. But that's not real life! We live in an imperfect world, and life isn't always going to be smooth and easy.

What can we do to help smooth out the rough spots in our paths, spiritually speaking? The only thing we can do is take our stand on God's Word by being "... *doers of the word, and not hearers only* ..." (James 1:22).

So many times we hear the Word and hear the Word, but eventually we have to *act on* God's Word. And we have to do it while the devil is using a great, big magnifying glass to magnify our problems.

If there's a gigantic obstacle blocking your path, just climb up on that stumbling block and declare, "I am more than a conqueror in Christ Jesus" (Rom. 8:37).

If a financial problem is looming before you, climb up on that bump and proclaim God's Word—"I can't go under for going over" (Mark 4:35)! Begin to declare by faith, "My God shall supply all my need, according to His riches in glory by Christ Jesus" (Phil. 4:19).

When discouragement and depression are hovering over your life, climb up on that stumbling stone and boldly proclaim, "The joy of the Lord is my strength" (Neh. 8:10).

If your body is racked by pain and sickness is threatening to take you out, you can stand up on that stumbling block and speak out your faith: "By the stripes of Jesus, I'm healed!" (1 Peter 2:24). If you have to get up on that bump and stay on it, just keep declaring God's Word *by faith*.

We've got to have tenacity in our faith! If we want to overcome the devil's obstacles, we have to stand firm on the foundation of God's Word. Second Timothy 2:19 says, *"God's truth stands firm like a great rock, and nothing can shake it . . ."* (TLB).

Whatever bumps or boulders are blocking your path, you can find a promise from God's Word to stand on and you can climb up on that stone and declare, "I'm standing on the Rock—the Rock Christ Jesus. My Rock never shakes. My Rock never crumbles. I'm on a solid Foundation. My Rock will put me over!"

That's how you climb on top of the negative circumstances in life. That's how you're not moved by what you see with your natural eyes. You can use those circumstances that the devil means for stumbling blocks as bumps to climb on— and they will take you higher and higher on God's path for your life.

The Devil Was Playing Havoc With Our Minds!

My husband, Ken, and I know what it's like for the devil to throw bumps and boulders across our path. We know what it's like for Satan to yell in our ears, "Your God is not going to help you this time! Why are you depending on Him?"

I'll never forget when we were first traveling in the ministry with my father-in-law, Brother Hagin. I suddenly discovered I was expecting our daughter, Denise. But, we had no money in our budget to cover having a new baby. Of course, we knew what God's Word says. We knew that Philippians 4:19 says, *"My God shall supply all your need according to his riches in glory by Christ Jesus."*

So we climbed up on that bump, that stumbling block, and stood on God's Word. And we also put action to our faith. Every time we had a few extra days between meetings, my husband would schedule services where he could preach and we could receive an offering. Then we would put our faith on the line and believe God for the extra money we needed for our new baby.

I remember one time when we had scheduled a three-day meeting in a particular church, but we had no idea how large the church was. We had decided to set our faith in agreement for God to give us a $300 offering during that meeting. (That would be comparable to about $3,000 in today's economy.)

You can imagine how shocked we were when only 25 people showed up for the first service. I'm not talking about 25 adults either. There were children in the crowd that night too!

When we looked at that tiny audience, the devil started playing havoc with our minds. We couldn't imagine how God was going to give us a $300 offering from such a small crowd.

But we never said a word to each other about our doubts or concerns. We knew that once we had put our faith in God's Word on the line, we had to keep declaring it. So we kept saying, "Thank You, God, that our needs are met according to Your riches in glory by Christ Jesus." And we kept thanking the Lord for a $300 offering.

In the natural, we hoped the crowd would pick up the second night. But the next evening, the only ones in the auditorium were the same 25 people.

By then, my mind was going wild. It seemed foolish for us to believe that we could receive a $300 offering from a crowd that small, even during a three-day meeting. But my faith was not in those people. My faith was in my Source, the Lord Jesus Christ.

The third night the crowd was about the same as the first two nights. After the service the pastor handed my husband an envelope with a check in it. Ken just said, "Thank you," and then he stuck the envelope in his pocket. But we could hardly wait to get back to our little motor home where we stayed during the crusades so we could open that envelope!

Ken took one look at that check and started shouting! The offering from that tiny crowd of people was $305!

That was one of the most thrilling moments of our lives, because we had put our faith on the line and God had met our need in spite of the overwhelming odds against it. It's so exciting to climb up on those bumps, those stumbling blocks, and watch God turn them into His miracle stepping-stones!

The Faith Walk Is Not a Walk of Ease

Not long after our daughter was born, my husband began, at the instruction of his dad, to launch RHEMA Bible

Training Center. It was a wonderful experience—a great adventure. It was a lot like birthing a baby!

It took every ounce of faith we had to believe for the RHEMA budget to be met each month. And in those days the budget for the Bible school was small compared to the budget we have today.

At the same time, Ken and I were struggling to believe God for our own personal finances. Little did those first Bible school students know that we had to believe for our needs just as they did. I remember so many days when my husband went to work without a cent in his pocket, which meant that he had to believe God for his lunch!

That first year wasn't easy for us, in many ways. We weren't eating steaks, and sometimes we weren't even eating hamburgers. But we had faith in God's Word that He would supply all of our needs, and He did.

Even though it was a tough year for us in the natural, it was one of our most miraculous years spiritually. And it was through all the rough bumps and rocky places that our faith in God's Word grew and was increased.

We had no idea at the time what the future held for RHEMA. And we never dreamed how much our faith had to increase in order for us to operate the Bible school over the years. But we learned an important faith lesson through those early experiences.

We learned that you have to believe for pennies before you can believe for dollars. You have to believe for dollars before you can believe for hundreds of dollars and thousands of dollars. Your faith doesn't grow overnight, but it does grow if you continue to use it.

During that time, Ken and I surrounded ourselves with the Word of God and saw miracles happen daily. There were times when we were almost down to our last dollar and there wasn't much food in the cupboard. Then my husband would burst through the door, saying, "Somebody just handed me $10," or, "I received $100 from so-and-so!"

Every time we ran into a bump in the road, one by one we climbed up on those bumps and stood on God's Word, and it was amazing how He met every need. He met not just a few of our needs, or most of our needs—but all of them! God had a great victory waiting for us on the other side of every stepping-stone.

Nobody Would Loan Us the Money

Ken and I encountered one of the biggest stumbling blocks of our lives during a large building project on the RHEMA campus—the construction of Student Development Centers 1 and 2. My husband had a big stack of invoices piled on his desk, and we didn't have enough money to cover them all. We desperately needed a loan, but no one would loan us any money.

The amount of money we had in the bank was more than the amount we needed to borrow, yet the bank still wouldn't give us a loan. So Satan began to yell in my husband's ears, "What are you going to do now? Your dad has turned the business side of the ministry over to you and you're going to take it down in only two years."

My husband just grabbed his Bible, walked over to his office window, and looked out across the RHEMA campus. Then he put his Bible on the floor, literally stood on it, and declared by faith, "Satan, my foot is on the Rock! I'm standing on God's Word, and we are going over. We're not going under!"

God showed Ken exactly what to do in that situation, and within 60 days every last bill was paid. Of course, we've had financial challenges since that time, but not once have we faced that same kind of challenge again. Do you know why? Because Satan knows he's not going to defeat us in that area.

I truly believe if you'll stand up to the challenges the devil throws across your path, he'll get tired of taking a whipping from you too! If you keep on beating him up with the power of God's Word, he's going to leave you alone in every area where you take your stand.

My Foot Is on the Rock

When Satan tries to stop you in your tracks, when he tries to deter you from accomplishing God's plan, you just tell him, "Mr. Devil, my foot is on the Rock—the Lord Jesus Christ—and I'm staying on that Rock. My heart is fixed on the Word of God, and the Word says my God will be with me in trouble, and He will deliver me" (Ps. 91:15).

It's so important for us to stand firm on the promises of God. I love the old hymn that says, "Standing on the promises that cannot fail, When the howling storms of doubt and fear assail, By the living Word of God I shall prevail, Standing on the promises of God!"[1]

Yes, it may get scary out there. I can tell you from my own experience, it *does* get scary out there. At times I've had to say, "Okay, God, this is too scary for me. I'm going to close my eyes and let You lead me."

But if you'll commit your whole way unto the Lord and put your trust in Him, He will lead you safely through the devil's minefield. It doesn't matter what bumps may fill your path or what obstacles may block your way. If you're holding on to the hand of the Lord Jesus Christ, He will lead you all the way to victory.

Make this declaration of your faith right now: *I'm standing on the Rock, the Rock Christ Jesus! He's the Rock that cannot be shaken, the Rock that never crumbles. I'm not going to leave that Rock. I'm determined to succeed in everything God has called me to do. I'm going to climb on top of every circumstance of life and turn the devil's stumbling blocks into my miracle stepping-stones!*

---

[1] R. Kelso Carter, 1886, "Standing on the Promises." Public Domain.

CHAPTER 3

'Lord, I Don't Want to Be a Missionary'

I remember as a little girl how terrified I was that God would call me to be a missionary. I wanted to be totally committed to the Lord, but I did not want to go to the mission field. Why? When the missionaries gave their testimonies at our church, they described how they had no electricity, no running water, no nothing!

I'm a city girl. I need electricity, running water, shopping malls, and restaurants. I was so afraid that if I committed my all to the Lord, He would ask me to be a missionary.

Every time we sang the song "I Surrender All," I would silently pray, "But, God, please don't ask me to be a missionary." And every time a missionary would come to our church, I would cry and cry. And as I wiped away the tears, I would tell God sincerely, "Lord, please don't call me to the mission field!"

Of course, I loved to hear the missionaries speak, and their stories touched my heart. But that made me even more afraid that God was calling me to be a missionary.

I'll never forget how the Lord finally set me free from my terrible fear of being called to the mission field. After my husband and I were married, a missionary spoke at our church. I was sitting there boo-hooing and thinking, *Oh, dear God, please don't call us to be missionaries!* when my husband said something that set my heart free. He said, "You can have a heart for missions without having a call for missions."

I thought, *That's why I cry every time I hear a missionary speak. I have a heart for missions, but thank God, I don't have a call for missions.*

The Lord may not ask us to be missionaries or do something else that we desperately don't want to do. But He still wants us to have a willing heart. He wants us to have a heart that's totally committed to Him. Sometimes we get so caught up in worrying about all the details of God's plan that we miss the whole point. Our Heavenly Father just wants us to be 100 percent committed to His will and His plan.

That means we have to do what Jesus did as He faced the Cross. We have to say, "God, not my will, but Thy will be done" (Luke 22:42). We have to commit our whole being to the Lord!

Abraham, Are You Willing?

One of the greatest examples in the Bible of someone who was totally committed to the Lord is found in the story of Abraham in Genesis chapter 22. In chapter 1 of this book we saw how Abraham left his homeland because God had said to him, "Go to a place I will show you" (Gen. 12:1). Abraham trusted the Lord so much that he committed himself to God's plan, even though he had no idea where God was taking him.

Later in his life, Abraham had to make a type of commitment that few of us will ever have to make. After God had given Abraham and Sarah their promised son, Isaac, the Lord told Abraham, "Take your only son, Isaac, and offer him to Me as a sacrifice."

Now, if you're a parent, you can imagine how you would feel if God said to you, "Give Me your child!" And, of course, God did *not* want Abraham to sacrifice his son to Him, and He is *not* asking you and me to sacrifice our children to Him either. He just wants us to be willing to do whatever He asks us to do.

Abraham didn't even hesitate to obey the Lord. He took his son Isaac and two of his servants to Mount Moriah where God had told him to make the sacrifice. Abraham told the servants, "You stay here, and Isaac and I will go up the mountain to worship. Then we'll come back to you again."

It must have torn a hole in Abraham's heart when Isaac asked him, "Father, where is the lamb for the sacrifice?"

But Abraham spoke words of faith when he said, "God will provide Himself a lamb."

After Abraham had built the altar and prepared to make his sacrifice, all of a sudden, the angel of the Lord called out to him and said, "Don't lay a hand on the boy!" Then God provided a ram for Abraham to sacrifice.

Did you notice that when Abraham was willing to give God his all, God didn't require Abraham to sacrifice everything to Him? What God required was a commitment to Him and a willingness on Abraham's part to obey. Isaiah 1:19 says, *"If you are willing and obedient, You shall eat the good of the land"* (NKJV). Because of Abraham's obedience and his willing heart, God poured out His blessings on every area of Abraham's life.

I Don't Want to Decorate

When I left my home and family in Texas and moved to Oklahoma so my husband could help his father in the ministry, I thought I had taken the ultimate step to prove how committed I was to the will of God. That was one of the hardest things I had ever done in my life.

After we arrived in Oklahoma and my husband began to help Brother Hagin establish RHEMA Bible Training Center, I began to seek the Lord about my role in the ministry at that time. As I poured out my heart to God in prayer, I told Him, "Lord, I want to do what You want me to do. I'm totally committed to You."

Of course, I had a whole list of things I thought God might call me to do. I'm a good organizer, so I thought He might ask me to help organize the ministry departments. I had also worked as a bookkeeper and had some business experience, so I thought the Lord might want me to use some of those gifts to help in the ministry.

Really, what it all boiled down to was this: I wanted to do what I was comfortable doing. But I was totally shocked when God asked me to do something that wasn't on my list!

You see, we were in the process of constructing several buildings on the RHEMA campus. One day my husband said to me, "Honey, we need somebody to choose the wallpaper, the carpet, and the paint for these buildings. We need someone to handle the decorating for RHEMA." And suddenly I knew that God wanted me to be that someone.

Have you ever noticed how, when we pray, "Lord, I'll do what You want me to do," we're usually expecting God to give us some great, big, important ministry? Then we're so surprised when the Lord says, "Go pick out wallpaper and carpet."

As soon as God opened that door, I began to argue with Him. "But, God, I'm not qualified to do that," I insisted. I had always been too busy to spend much time decorating our house. Sometimes I hung pictures on the walls, but that was about the extent of my decorating experience. So I said, "God, I don't know how to choose carpet and wallpaper!"

I'll never forget as long as I live what the Lord said to me next. "That's your problem, Lynette. You want to rely on your ability, your sufficiency, instead of on My ability. In yourself, there's no way you can do what I'm asking you to do. But I'm going to teach you how to listen to My voice. That's the only way you're going to be able to complete all the assignments I have for you in life."

"Okay, Lord," I replied. "This is definitely going to have to be a supernatural decorating job!" That was when I first adopted Philippians 4:13 as the verse I live by every day—"*I can do all things through Christ who strengthens me*" (NKJV).

As I began to "decorate" RHEMA, at times I woke up in the middle of the night in a cold sweat because I was having nightmares about the projects I was working on. In my dreams, I saw a big crowd of people gathered in an auditorium I had decorated, and they were saying, "Ooooh, who decorated this place? It looks awful!"

My new decorating job was a huge challenge, but I was so happy to be doing something for the Lord. One piece at a time, I chose the wallpaper, the paint, the carpet, and the furniture. And as I made those decisions, I learned how to listen to the voice of God.

I didn't know that RHEMA was going to grow bigger and bigger, and so was my decorating job. I just tackled one task after another, from selecting the carpet for a massive auditorium to choosing the paint for all the campus buildings. And my heart's cry was, "Lord, I'll do what You want me to do, but please give me a strong anointing to do it."

It was important to me for the atmosphere in those buildings to be warm and inviting—especially in the RHEMA Bible Church building. A church is a place where people gather to worship the Lord, and you want a church building to feel warm and comfortable.

One day the company that had sold us some of our carpet sent their decorators to look at the lobby of one of the buildings I had decorated. It was such a blessing to me when I heard one of them exclaim, "This is beautiful! It feels so warm in here!" I knew they weren't bragging on me. They were bragging on my God!

You see, His abilities are so much greater than our abilities. I thank God for His ability that's working on the inside of us. If we truly want to accomplish what He's called us to do, we have to lean on the anointing and the ability of the Lord.

God's To-Do List

Sometimes we get so focused on our own plans and agendas that we forget to ask God, "What is Your agenda, Lord?" We have such long to-do lists that there's no time left to pray or read the Bible or worship the Lord.

One thing I am in life is persistent. Once I start a task, I don't want to stop until I'm finished. Nothing or no one is going to interrupt me—sometimes not even God Himself!

My daughter, Denise, can testify to this. She'll never let me live down what happened one morning when she had an appendicitis attack. I was in the middle of putting on my makeup when she began to experience excruciating pain. It was on the weekend and we happened to know the doctor personally, so he came by our house to check on her.

"She's having an appendicitis attack," he told us. "You need to get her to the hospital. I'll meet you there."

So I said to her, "Honey, we'll go to the hospital, but first I've got to finish putting on my makeup." (This really happened!)

Oh dear! Sometimes we get so focused on our to-do lists that God can hardly get through to us if He has something else He wants us to do.

Thank goodness, Denise made it through that appendicitis attack in spite of my being so focused on getting my tasks done. But that was a good opportunity for me to see whose plan I was committed to—my plan or God's plan.

I believe it's important for us to stay focused and accomplish the tasks on our to-do lists. But it's even more important for us to listen to the voice of God and be sensitive to Him when He wants us to change our plans or go in a different direction.

You see, when we talk about committing ourselves to God's plan, we're usually thinking about the big things in life. We're thinking about Abraham's commitment to the Lord or someone answering God's call to be a missionary.

But we have all kinds of opportunities to show our commitment to the Lord every day. Do we allow Him to interrupt our busy schedules to minister to someone or just to talk with Him? And what about the opportunities we have to simply obey His Word? It takes commitment for us to do what God tells us in His Word.

For example, what do we do when someone wrongs us? Do we follow our will or God's will? In the natural, we want to give that person a piece of our mind, don't we? We want to get even and hold a grudge.

But when we're committed to doing God's will, we do what God's Word says. Instead of giving that person an earful, we do what Jesus said to do in Luke 6:28: *"Bless them that curse you, and pray for them which despitefully use you."*

I know that when I've been wronged or people have said hurtful things about me, sometimes I've wanted to cry because it hurt so much. The first thing I wanted to do was tell them off!

But I've chosen to do God's will and not mine. I've chosen to walk in love and get down on my knees and pray for the people who have wronged me, hurt me, or persecuted me.

It hasn't been easy to do, but I always remind myself that if I obey God's Word, He will be my Defense. And if I'll run to Him in my time of trouble, He will not only defend me, but He'll bring me through every challenge victoriously!

One Hundred Percent Sold Out to God

Are you committed to doing whatever the Lord wants you to do? Are you committed to allowing the interruptions He brings into your life? Or are you so busy checking off the items on your to-do list, your "mission accomplished" list, that there's no time left for God's to-do list?

God is saying to us, "Give Me your all"—not 80 percent, not 90 percent, but 100 percent sold out to Him!

For years I thought I was fully committed to the Lord, but there was still this little 5 percent of my life that I wanted to keep for myself. Finally, when I was at my lowest point, I said, "God, whatever You want me to do is okay with me. I'm going to stop trying to plan my life and let You plan it for me." When I committed a full 100 percent to the Lord, He led me on a path that was beyond anything I had ever dreamed of.

It's the most exciting thing in the world to live for God, but it's even more exciting when you're 100 percent committed to Him. It's a great adventure—an amazing journey. And He has a mighty work for us to do if we'll follow Him *with all of our hearts*!

CHAPTER 4

THE ANT WHO CARRIED
THE CONTACT LENS

I want to tell you a story—a true story—about a young woman named Brenda who was invited by some of her friends to go rock climbing. Although she was terrified of heights, she went with them to a huge granite cliff. After she put on her climbing gear, she took a deep breath, grabbed hold of the rope, and started up the face of that rock.

It seemed like forever before she finally reached a ledge where she could take a breather. As she was poised there in midair, the safety rope snapped across her face and one of her contact lenses popped out. Now, you may not know how that feels, but I wear contact lenses so I know how upsetting it can be to lose a contact!

There Brenda was, clinging to a rock ledge, with hundreds of feet of sheer cliff above her and hundreds of feet below her, and one missing contact lens. On top of that, her sight was beginning to get blurry.

In desperation, she started searching all over that ledge for her contact lens, but it was nowhere to be found. Suddenly fear began to grip her heart. She cried out to the Lord and asked Him to help her find the missing contact.

At last Brenda reached the top of the cliff, and one of her friends examined her eye and clothing to see if she could find the contact lens. But there was still no sign of it. As Brenda sat there waiting for the rest of her group to reach the top, she continued to pour out her heart to the Lord in prayer.

Looking out across that beautiful range of mountains, she said, "God, Your Word says that the eyes of the Lord run to and fro throughout the whole earth. You can see all of these mountains. You know every stone and leaf, and You know exactly where my contact lens is. Please help me find it!"

Finally, she and her group went back down to the bottom of the cliff where a new party of climbers was waiting to go up. One of them shouted, "Hey, has anybody lost a contact lens?"

It was startling enough that somebody had found a contact lens—those things are tiny! But do you know why that climber spotted Brenda's contact lens? An ant was slowly crawling across the face of the rock, dragging Brenda's contact along with him. An ant carrying a contact lens! Can you picture that?

Later Brenda told her father, who is a cartoonist, this unusual story and he drew a cartoon of an ant carrying a contact lens. The caption read: "Lord, I don't know why You want me to carry this thing. I can't eat it and it's awfully heavy. But if this is what You want me to do, I'll carry it for You!"

That story tells me that God loves us so much that He will do whatever is necessary to answer our prayers. If He caused an ant to carry a contact lens across a granite cliff to answer Brenda's prayers, then He will move Heaven and earth to answer your prayers and mine. If we really believe that's true, it will be so much easier for us *to believe* when we pray!

Lord, Help Me Find a Job

I remember a prayer God answered for me when my husband and I were first married. Ken was a young preacher, and he was accepting every speaking engagement that came along. But sometimes the invitations were few and far between. Meanwhile, the company I worked for closed their office in the town where we lived, so I was out of a job.

Here we were, young newlyweds with no consistent income. So I began to pray and ask the Lord to help me find a new job. And every time I went on an interview, I prayed for God to give me favor.

There was one particular job I applied for that had to do with calculating the job performances of the people who worked on an assembly line. During the interview, the man asked me, "Do you have any experience using a calculator? Can you operate a calculator by touch?"

My heart sank. I'm good with math, but I had never used a calculator. I knew what one looked like, but this company was interested in speed, and I certainly didn't have any speed in using a calculator!

So I was honest with the man. I didn't tell him that I had a skill which I did not possess. Instead, I said, "No, sir, I don't have any experience using a calculator. But I'm excellent at math, and I'm a quick learner. I'm confident that, with just a little bit of training, I can do a good job for you." No, I wasn't confident in myself—I was confident in the Greater One, the Holy Spirit, Who lives on the inside of me!

Do you know what? That man hired me over other applicants who were more qualified than I was. I believe that happened because I had prayed for favor. You see, my Heavenly Father has promised me in His Word that He will surround me with favor (Ps. 5:12).

Not only that, but I became a great employee for that company. With the Holy Spirit's help, I became faster on my job than anybody else who worked there—even the ones who had years of experience.

High Heels and Handkerchiefs:
Learning to Pray With the Prayer Warriors

All of my life I have loved to pray. When I was only 2 years old, my mother found me in her bedroom one day, praying my heart out. I had gotten into her closet, put on a pair of her high heels, and found a handkerchief, and I was clutching that handkerchief and imitating the ladies I had seen at our church as they prayed around the altar.

She watched in amazement while I knelt down by the bed, praying and dabbing my eyes with that little handkerchief because that's what I had seen the prayer warriors at our church do as they prayed and cried out to the Lord.

One reason prayer was so important to me was, I was a timid, quiet child. I didn't express my thoughts, opinions, and deepest feelings very easily. To be honest, I didn't want to expose my feelings to others because I was afraid of their reaction. The only Person I talked to about those things was the Lord, and when I was very young, He became my best friend.

Anytime I had a need, I would talk to my Heavenly Father. When I was taking a test at school, I would talk to God about it. When I had to do something that was difficult for me, I would always talk to the Lord. I grew up believing that whenever I had a need, all I had to do was ask my Heavenly Father, and He would supply my needs.

Really, that's what I've done all of my life, and that's why the Lord is so dear to me today. He's always been there for me, and to this day He is still my very best friend!

As I was growing up, my prayer life was greatly influenced by a precious relative of mine, Aunt Oma. She was an amazing prayer warrior. I mean, if you asked Aunt Oma to pray about something, you had better want an answer because she always got her answers from the Lord!

Aunt Oma never married and had children, but she dearly loved children. And she loved to plant the desire for

God in children's hearts. I have many wonderful memories of Aunt Oma taking me home with her when I was little and teaching me the Word. While the other children were out playing, I was in Aunt Oma's living room, memorizing scriptures.

She would say to me, "Honey, it's so important for you to hide God's Word in your heart." And then she would help me learn one verse after another from the Bible.

My aunt's prayer life was something else! One of the things I remember the most about Aunt Oma's prayers was that she prayed loudly and fervently. I guess she wanted to make sure that her Heavenly Father heard her, and she wanted to make doubly sure that the devil heard her too.

As I watched Aunt Oma pray, I began to realize what a dynamic force prayer was in her life. It was through her example that I developed a real heart for prayer and a persistency in prayer.

I remember one time when I was about 6 years old, I was over at Aunt Oma's house. We didn't have a lot of toys in those days, so we had to make our own toys. I desperately wanted to make a swing in the big mulberry tree in Aunt Oma's yard. So I asked her, "Can we go to the store and get some chain to make a swing?" Now this was Saturday afternoon and the stores closed at 6 o'clock.

So Aunt Oma took me from one hardware store to the next, but we couldn't seem to find any chain. It was almost

6 o'clock when we arrived at yet another hardware store, and she said to me, "Honey, the stores are closing now. This is the last store we can go to. If we can't get the chain this weekend, we'll get it the next time you come to visit."

Well, I wasn't satisfied with that idea so I started praying. I said, "God, You know how much I want this swing. Please let this store have some chain." Lo and behold, when my aunt walked out of that store, she was carrying some chain for my swing!

Really, I didn't have any doubt that God was going to answer my prayer! Why? Because I had already learned, even at that young age, to trust the Lord. I had learned how faithful He is. And, above all, I had learned how much He cares about me. And He doesn't care about me any more than He cares about you!

Acts 10:34 says that God is not a respecter of persons. In other words, He doesn't play favorites. Sometimes we question God's love for us because of some kind of negative experience we've had in the past. But if we don't believe God really cares about us, how can we believe that He's going to answer our prayers?

The most important factor in having a powerful, effective prayer life is knowing our Heavenly Father. The more that we get to know Him, the more we'll realize how much He loves us and how dear we are to Him. It's important for us to realize how precious we are to the Lord, not because of anything special we've done, but because we're His very own children!

We respond to the heart cries of our children, don't we? If they're in trouble and they start hollering, "Help!" what do we do? We help them. Our Heavenly Father loves us so much more than we can possibly imagine, and He's always ready to answer our cries!

Communing With the Father

You may be thinking, *But Lynette, I don't have the same kind of relationship with the Father that you have.* But you can! He desperately wants to have that kind of relationship with you.

How can we develop a closer relationship with the Lord? First of all, we can get to know Him better by reading and meditating on His Word. There's so much we can learn about what God is like when we read and study the Bible. And if we want Him to answer our prayers, we need to know what He's promised us in His Word.

We can also get to know our Heavenly Father by spending time with Him in prayer. How do we develop a relationship with *anyone* in our lives? We spend time with them, don't we? We communicate with them. We talk with them and they talk with us. One of the best ways I know of for us to develop our relationship with the Lord is just to spend time communicating with Him in prayer.

And remember, God doesn't want our prayer time to be something stiff or formal. He wants us to feel comfortable with Him—as if we're sitting in our living room, talking with our dearest friend.

Don't be concerned if it takes a little time for you to develop the close communication you desire with your Heavenly Father. Even in the natural, communication takes time to develop. When my husband and I were first married, we had to learn to communicate with each other. And it's taken time for us to develop good communication. Now that we've been together over 40 years, we've learned how to communicate so well that we've even started to think alike!

It's the same way in our relationship with our Heavenly Father. Just because we've given our hearts to the Lord doesn't mean that our communication system with Him has been perfected. We need to commune with Him and learn how to hear His voice. And the more we pray and see Him answer our prayers, the more confidence we'll have that He's going to answer us in the future.

A Miracle Answer to Prayer

I remember another prayer God answered for Ken and me in the early days of our marriage. It was in 1969, and I was expecting our son, Craig. We were driving an old car that seemed to be broken down more often than it was running. We couldn't afford the payments on a new car, but our old car was in such bad shape that we never knew if it was going to make it from one stop to the next.

To top things off, it was summertime, and the air conditioner in our car wasn't working. Ken's uncle had already fixed it several times, but he finally told us not to bring it back because it wasn't worth fixing. We were praying for a new car, but there seemed to be no way, in the natural, for God to answer our prayers.

Then a wonderful miracle happened. A woman of some financial means got hold of a copy of Brother Hagin's book *The Believer's Authority.* She was reading it during an airplane flight when the plane suddenly started to plunge to the earth. This woman decided to put what she had read into action. She began to exercise her authority as a believer in that situation, and the plane did not crash!

Later, when she told Brother Hagin her testimony, she asked him an odd question. She said, "Do you have a son?"

"Yes," Brother Hagin told her, "I have a son."

Then she asked, "Well, does he need a car?"

Brother Hagin quickly let this woman know how desperately we needed a car. So we met with her and she told us, "God has told me to give you a car. Just go to the dealership and pick out whatever car you want, and I'll pay for it."

We picked out a brand-new, gold Oldsmobile, and it was absolutely beautiful. It cost $4,800, a lot of money in those days, and we were thrilled with that car. We got it about a week before our son was born, and my husband was so excited over his new car and his new son that he forgot to fill up the gas tank when he was driving back and forth to the hospital. We were on our way home from the hospital with our new baby when our brand-new car suddenly sputtered to a stop—completely out of gas!

What a blessing it was that all we had to do to get that car running again was put some gas in it. We were so grateful to the Lord for answering our prayers.

The World Needs Our Prayers

The world today is in such turmoil, and there are so many things God wants us to pray about. Not only does He desire for us to pray about our own personal needs, but I also believe He wants us to pray about other situations around us.

First Peter 4:7 says, *"But the end of all things is at hand: be ye therefore sober, and watch unto prayer."* The *New Living Translation* puts it this way: *"The end of the world is coming soon. Therefore, be earnest and disciplined in your prayers."*

In 2002, not long after the 9/11 terrorist attacks on America, snipers in several areas were randomly killing people. Because of the huge tragedy our country had just gone through, fear suddenly began to grip the nation.

On the Sunday night before the snipers were caught, I was conducting a prayer service in our church. By the inspiration of the Holy Spirit, I said, "I think we need to pray that those snipers will be caught." We joined together as a congregation in prayer, and we believed the snipers would be caught, and quickly!

Later I read a story about a group of Christian truckers who also prayed about that situation. One particular trucker who was scheduled to retire at the time felt sure God was going to answer their prayers. In fact, he told the others at the prayer meeting, "I believe God is going to use me in this situation."

A few days later, as this trucker was driving down the road, listening to a report about the snipers on his radio, all at once he felt compelled to pull off the highway into a rest stop. This rest stop just happened to be a few miles from where that prayer meeting took place. As he pulled into the rest stop, he was shocked to see a car in the parking lot that was similar to the vehicle the authorities believed the snipers were driving.

A chill rushed down his spine as he read the number on the license plate. The tag number of that car matched the license plate number that was given on the radio. He quickly called 911 and then he used his truck to block the exit ramp so no one could escape.

That trucker said later that those were the longest 15 minutes of his life as he waited for the police to arrive on the scene. But thank God, the snipers were caught that day, and I believe they were caught because of the power of prayer.

Don't Worry About Praying Eloquent Prayers

If we only realized how powerful our prayers are, I believe we would be much more excited about praying. In fact, we would probably want to pray all the time because we would always expect to get results!

James 5:16 says, "*The earnest prayer of a righteous person has great power and produces wonderful results*" (NLT). A righteous person is someone who is in right standing with God, someone who has given his or her heart to the Lord.

I believe the Lord wants to build up our confidence in the power of our prayers and stir us up to pray. He wants us to be more dedicated and serious about our prayer life than we've ever been. Why? Because this world desperately needs our prayers!

And He doesn't want us to worry about how eloquent our prayers are. He doesn't want us to use any big, fancy words when we pray. Our Heavenly Father just wants us to talk to Him as we would talk to the most wonderful daddy in the world. And He wants us to remember that His hand is always open to us, His children, and His ears are always open to our cries.

CHAPTER 5

THE HOLY GHOST KNOWS

Ever since I was a little girl, I've had a hunger for the Lord and for the moving of His Spirit. I can remember going to the altar even at the age of 4 to pray with the adults when they gathered there.

In those days, we had long church conferences and meetings. They weren't just three-day conferences as we have today. They were three-week meetings! And the services didn't start at 7:00 p.m. and end at 9:00 or even 10:00 p.m. like today's services. They started at 7:45 p.m. and lasted until after midnight, because we didn't think the Holy Ghost could move until after midnight.

Where did we get that idea? We got it from the story of Paul and Silas in Acts chapter 16. If you remember, Paul and Silas were singing praises to God at midnight in a jail cell. Suddenly the foundations of the prison began to rattle and shake, and God began to move in that jail cell at midnight!

I grew up in a Pentecostal church, and we loved the moving of God's Spirit. We didn't have nurseries or children's church services when I was a child, so I sat right there on the pew, night after night, service after service. Even if I fell asleep, my little spirit was still soaking up the things of God.

I believe God was laying a foundation in my heart during my early years to help me follow the leading of the Spirit, so I wouldn't get away from that as I grew older. Proverbs 22:6 says, *"Train up a child in the way he should go, And when he is old he will not depart from it"* (NKJV).

I'm so thankful that our children had the same kind of foundation in the Holy Ghost that my husband and I both had. When our son, Craig, was only 3 years old, we began traveling with Brother Hagin in his crusades. There were no nurseries, so Craig just sat in the services and played quietly. I brought little cars for him to play with and crayons so he could color. But even while he was playing, he was absorbing the Word of God and becoming sensitive to the moving of the Holy Spirit.

It was always amazing to me how Craig would be playing with his cars or coloring quietly, when all of a sudden, he would begin to pick up his toys and whisper, "Pa Pa's about to close." There was no indication to the rest of us that Brother Hagin was about to close the service. But Craig's little spirit was so sensitive to the Holy Spirit that he realized when his grandfather was about to close.

Craig wanted to know when Pa Pa was going to close a service because he was fascinated by watching him pray for the sick. To this day, Craig loves to minister to the sick and pray for people in the healing lines.

Our daughter, Denise, was only 8 weeks old when she started traveling with us in the crusades. I believe she was absorbing the things of God even as she lay in her little cradle, sleeping beside the piano bench while I played for the services. All she ever knew was church.

I'll never forget one time when she was a little girl, I heard her say to her brother, "Bubby, let's play church."

My ears really perked up when I heard that, because I thought, *I want to see what stands out the most to her about church.*

I heard her tell Craig, "I'm going to pray for the sick and you be my 'catcher.'" In other words, she wanted him to catch whoever she prayed for if they fell under the power of God.

Denise's "sick people" were her three stuffed bunnies—Fluffy, Nuffy, and Stuffy. I peeked around the corner just in time to see her set those little bunnies all in a row while Craig stood right behind them, holding them very carefully. Then she laid her hands on each bunny, one at a time, and said, "Be healed in the Name of Jesus!"

After she had prayed for a bunny, she would knock it over and say, "Pshew!" just as she had heard her grandfather say when he prayed for people in healing lines. Of course, Craig was standing by the whole time, ready to catch those bunnies before their little paws could touch the floor!

All Craig and Denise ever knew was the moving of the Holy Spirit and the power of God. And thank God, they learned at an early age how to be sensitive to the Spirit!

Lord, I Really Do Need a Personal GPS

To accomplish what God wants us to in these last days, we're going to have to be sensitive to what the Holy Spirit is saying to our spirits. You see, God's Spirit can lead us and guide us like a supernatural GPS—a personal navigation system.

Just as a GPS can help you locate a street or address in a city or town, the Holy Spirit can help you follow the route God has planned for your life. And He can help you avoid some of the hidden dangers that are on the road ahead.

I remember an incident that illustrates what I'm talking about here. My best friend, Lanell, was helping me with one of our conferences at RHEMA Bible Church. She had grabbed a big armload of things just as she was about to step down off the platform.

Suddenly, something on the inside of her said, "Don't go down those steps. Don't carry all of that stuff." But she ignored that little warning because it sounded weird to her.

Well, guess what? She fell down the steps! By the grace of God she didn't hurt herself too badly, but the Holy Spirit had been trying to warn her so she wouldn't get hurt at all. And the Spirit of God will try to warn us too. It's so important for us not to ignore the warning of the Spirit.

My husband has an unusual way of describing the feeling that he often gets when the Holy Spirit is trying to give him some kind of warning. He says it feels as if something is "scratching down on the inside." Don't ignore that feeling down in your spirit, because if you do, you're going to get into trouble.

I remember one time years ago when my husband and I really did need a personal GPS, in the natural. It was before we moved to Tulsa, and we were just passing through town on our way to St. Louis. My husband thought he knew a shortcut to get to the interstate, but we wound up roaming around Tulsa, Oklahoma, for over two hours!

The "shortcut" that was supposed to get us to St. Louis by noon delayed our arrival there until 5 o'clock in the afternoon. And sometimes that's the way it is in life. What we think is a shortcut can become the long way around, and then we try to blame God for the delay. But God is not the problem. Those kinds of delays and detours happen because we've overlooked the little warnings and nudges from the Holy Spirit.

How can we learn to be more sensitive to God's Spirit? How can we get our spiritual GPS tuned in to the Lord?

One of the best ways I know of to learn how to hear God's voice and follow the leading of His Spirit is by doing what I talked about in the last chapter—getting better acquainted with our Heavenly Father through His Word and prayer. As we read what the Bible says about Jesus, we can get to know what our Heavenly Father is like, because Jesus said, *"If you have seen me, you have seen the Father"* (John 14:9 CEV). And we can learn more about the nature of God and how He operates as we read and study His entire Word.

Also, the more time we spend in prayer, communing with the Lord, the better we can hear His voice. Even if we don't have time to pray for hours on end, we can stay in an attitude of prayer and commune with the Lord all day long.

I try to stay tuned in to my Heavenly Father as I go about my daily tasks—my natural, normal activities. I pray and praise God while I'm getting ready for work and while I'm driving down the road in my car. The more I stay tuned in to the Lord during my daily activities, the more sensitive I am to the Holy Spirit's voice.

In our hectic world, we desperately need to stay aware of God's Spirit. We need to hear His voice. It's so important for us to have our spiritual GPS system constantly tuned in to the Lord!

Hearing From God When You Least Expect It

When I need a strong word from the Lord, sometimes I'll hear from Him at a moment when I'm not even thinking about it. If I've been praying and meditating about something and seeking God's will, I may get the answer I need from Him when I'm doing something totally unrelated.

I remember one time years ago when we had some hard decisions to make in our ministry. I had been seeking the Lord about those things, but I still wasn't certain which way to go.

My husband and I had decided to take our kids on a little four-wheeling trip, and I had been riding really hard that day. We were going through all of those "whoopsie-dos"—the bumps out on the trail—when suddenly I stopped at the top of a sand dune to look at the beautiful scenery.

I was just sitting there, quietly praising the Lord, when all at once God began to give me the answers to those hard questions I had been asking Him about for months. Those answers came at a time when I wasn't even thinking about it.

Of course, we need to pray and seek God continually for His answers and direction. But sometimes we concentrate so hard on trying to hear from Him that our hearts are not open to receive His answers. Or we may be so busy telling God what we need that we can't hear what He's saying to us.

It's kind of like having a conversation with someone, but we're talking so much that we can't hear a word the other person is saying. We tell God what we need and want, and we give Him a long list of questions we want Him to answer. But instead of waiting for His reply, we rush off to our next task and don't hear what our Heavenly Father wants to say to us.

It's important for us to learn to wait on the Lord, to wait for His answers. But we also need to remember that God can speak to us at any moment—even at the most unusual times—if we'll keep our hearts open to Him.

Thinking Out Loud

I remember how frustrated I used to get while waiting for a decision from my father-in-law concerning something I was responsible for in our ministry. There were times when he would say to me, "I think we should go this way," but then he would quickly add, "Now, I'm just thinking out loud."

Then he would meditate some more about that decision and later he would come back to me and say, "No, we don't have it exactly right." Why did he do that? Because God may not give us the answers we need all at once.

Do you remember what happened in First Samuel chapter 16 when God sent the prophet Samuel to anoint David to be king over Israel? How many of Jesse's sons did Samuel go through before he finally found the right one? Seven! After the prophet had looked at all the sons except David, he asked Jesse, "Are all of your children here?" or, "Don't you have any more sons?"

"Oh yes," Jesse replied. "I've got one more, but he's out in the field." Then he added, "He's young," meaning, "He's not qualified for this job." But thank God, the Lord doesn't always follow the "qualified" plan. Instead, He qualifies the plan He chooses. When David was brought before Samuel, the prophet anointed that young, unqualified shepherd boy to be the new king of Israel!

Notice that God didn't give Samuel the answer all at once about whom He wanted to be king. And He may not give us the answers we need all at once either.

When Brother Hagin was "thinking out loud," he was really giving the Lord the opportunity to reveal the answers to him, step by step. And I learned in those situations not to move on anything until he came back to me again. Then I would repeat the decision, the plan, exactly as I understood it and ask him, "Is this what you want us to do?" When he confirmed it, I would go with that plan.

Through those experiences, I came to realize that there are times when God may not confirm something to us until we speak it out loud—until we "think out loud" about it. And sometimes it's only when we speak something out loud that God lets us know we're not supposed to go in that direction.

Of course, we need to be careful about who we share those things with. It's probably best not to share them with anyone besides our spouse or perhaps a close friend. And we also need to let that person know that we don't want them to tell anyone else about it.

So many times over the years, we have gone through this process of "weighing" something in our spirits, and then we've suddenly realized that we were about to go in the wrong direction. In some cases, going in the direction we had originally planned could have been disastrous. That's why it's absolutely necessary for us to stay tuned in to the Holy Spirit.

Warnings and Alarm Bells

When my husband and I were first married, Ken had just gotten out of the United States Army after serving for three years. He didn't have any bills, but he didn't have any money either. In fact, he only had about three dollars to his name! I had a job, but I also had bills.

Even after he started working as an associate pastor for my dad, Rev. V.E. Tipton, our total monthly income was still only $200. We were barely getting by.

Then one day I came home from work, and Ken met me with a big smile. "Guess what, honey!" he said excitedly. "I just received a telegram from the United States government."

"Really! What did it say?" I asked.

"Well, it's about a job opportunity, and we can travel all over the world." Ken loves to travel, and this job sounded wonderful. The government wanted to interview him right away and they were eager to offer him the job.

Then he added, "The starting salary is $15,000 a year!" Now, this was 1966. We were making $2,400 a year with both of us working. This job would pay $15,000 and I wouldn't have to work!

Do you think that job was a temptation to us? I guarantee you, it was—a huge temptation! I thought, *Oh, wow! No more money problems.*

Of course, my husband was extremely excited about this opportunity, because he desperately wanted to be a good provider for his new bride. Really, he wanted to be my hero! "Oh, honey," he sighed. "That would be wonderful, wouldn't it? I'm going to go check out this job."

All of a sudden—thank God for the Holy Ghost—something on the inside of me rose up like an alarm. I mean, I had such a strong warning in my spirit that I knew he shouldn't even go check out that job!

"Now, I'm not going to take the job," he told me. "I know I'm called to be in the ministry. But I just want to check it out." By that time, it was as if the devil himself was tantalizing my husband with this temptation.

To be honest, I'm not an extremely demonstrative person. But all at once the words just flew out of my mouth, "No, you're not going to check out that job!" And instantly, we were having our first argument!

"Well, why not?" he asked me. "I'm not going to take the job. I'm just going to check it out."

"No, you're not!" I insisted.

"Yes, I am!"

Just as I started to leave the room, I blurted out, "I want to tell you one thing. I married a preacher, and I intend to live with a preacher!"

My husband was dumbfounded, but he listened and did not check out that job. I'm so thankful that the Holy Spirit warned us not to take that job, and I'm also thankful that my husband listened to the warning. It's important for us to be sensitive to God's warnings and alarm bells, but it's also important for us to be quick to obey.

Waking Up the Whole House

In most cases, I believe God reveals His plan for our lives one step at a time. But there are times when He may reveal to us a definite long-range plan. Many years ago the Lord revealed a plan to my husband and me that covered a number of years.

It happened right after we went to work for his dad in the ministry. We were between crusades and were staying with my father- and mother-in-law. It was late, and my husband had already drifted off to sleep when the spirit of prayer suddenly came upon me. I began to pray very quietly in the Spirit, and then I started to interpret what I was praying in English.

When my husband tells this story, he says that as he lay there, fast asleep, all at once he heard this booming voice—my voice—and his first thought was, *My wife is hollering so loudly that she's going to wake up the whole house!* When he actually awakened, he realized that I was praying quietly, almost in a whisper.

We were both a little discouraged at the time, because we didn't understand why God wanted us to go to work for his dad in the ministry. We knew in our spirits it was what we were supposed to do, but in the natural, our heads were giving us some problems.

As I began to interpret the words the Lord was giving me to encourage us, what came out of my mouth was so astounding that I didn't even believe it myself. As we sat there in that bedroom praying, the Holy Spirit unfolded the plan of God for our lives for the next 20 years. He showed us wonderful, amazing things—things we had never dreamed of. And one by one, the things that He told us have come to pass.

Those things didn't happen overnight. They didn't happen in 5 years, or 10 years, or even 15 years. We had every opportunity to take our eyes off the goal or veer to the right or to the left. But we stayed on track because we knew we were following God's plan.

When you follow God's plan for your life, the Holy Spirit will give you peace. Yes, there will be challenges. There will be times when your mind will give you fits. But there will also be peace—a peace in your heart that passes all human understanding.

Of course, when God reveals a long-range plan to us, we still have to walk out the plan, step by step. Sometimes we're tempted to jump from step one to step five, but that's not how God planned it. He planned our futures *one step at a time*!

Go to the Word

I remember a difficult time in my life when we were changing directions in our ministry. In my search for God's wisdom and guidance for that situation, I had prayed and prayed and was seeking the Lord with all of my heart.

I wanted so badly to hear an audible "Thus saith the Lord," but that audible voice didn't come. I didn't even hear the still, small voice of the Holy Spirit speaking to me. So I began to say, "Where are You, God? I need to hear Your voice!"

I was so amazed by what I heard the Holy Spirit say in my spirit. He told me, "Go to the Word of God." Well, that wasn't exactly what I expected to hear! But thank God, we can always go to the Word for wisdom and guidance, and His Word will minister life to us.

Through the Word, God confirmed to me that the road we were taking was the right path. And that assurance in my spirit kept me steady during the tough times. God's Word has the power to keep us strong and lift our spirits, even during the most discouraging times in life. And above all, it's important for us to remember that the Holy Spirit will never lead us in a direction that's contrary to God's Word.

Decisions, Decisions, Decisions

In the day in which we live, we all face many decisions every day. That's why it's absolutely vital for us to find out which way the Holy Spirit is leading us to go.

God can speak to us in many different ways: through the inward witness or inner prompting of the Holy Spirit (Rom. 8:16); through His Word; through other people; through circumstances; through that little "scratching" feeling down on the inside; through the still, small voice of the Spirit speaking in our spirits; and even through the authoritative, "audible" voice of God.

Sometimes God speaks to you just through a feeling in your spirit that "something isn't right." Have you ever been in a situation where things seemed wonderful on the surface, but you didn't have any peace down on the inside? That was the Holy Spirit trying to tell you not to take that path!

Proverbs 20:27 says, *"The spirit of man is the candle of the Lord...."* A candle produces light, doesn't it? The Holy Spirit will light the way for you through your spirit, and He'll help you with every decision you make.

Thank God for the Holy Ghost inside us! He's been given to lead us, guide us, direct us, and keep us on the right path. And if we're going to fulfill our destiny and accomplish God's plan, we need to listen to the Holy Spirit with all of our hearts!

CHAPTER 6

THE PIN THAT
DROPPED FROM HEAVEN

In the middle of the night in January of 1983, Ken and I were jolted out of our sleep by an awful scream coming from our son's bedroom. My husband stumbled up the stairs, groggy, only to find our son, Craig, lying on the floor, holding his head, and crying out, "My head! My head!"

Craig was in the 8th grade at the time, and we had taken him to the doctor a few weeks earlier because he had been suffering from headaches. They had run several tests and had also taken X-rays, but they couldn't find anything wrong with him.

The doctor thought his sinuses might be causing the problem, but somehow on the inside of me I knew that something was desperately wrong. Our son just wasn't the happy child he normally was.

After we prayed for him that night, he finally drifted off to sleep. But the next day we took him back to the doctor, and they ran some more tests. I'll never forget the awful feeling I had in the pit of my stomach when five doctors surrounded us and gave us the shattering news: "Your son has a tumor the size of a large lemon that's pressing against his brain stem. Just one blow to his head could end his life."

(The scariest thing about the whole situation was that Craig was playing contact football at the time. At the very next game he was scheduled to play on the first string, which meant he would have been involved in a whole lot of rough contact!)

At that moment, nothing on this earth—houses, cars, or any other material possessions—mattered to us but the life of our son. For the first time in my life, I caught a glimpse of how God must have felt when He sacrificed His Son, Jesus, on the Cross. I thought, *Lord, why can't I take my son's place? God, why does it have to be my precious baby?*

Of course, we prayed with all of our hearts and stood firmly on God's Word as we believed for Craig's healing. Our families and friends prayed with us, but there was no immediate change in our son's condition. Then my father-in-law said something very powerful to us. He told us, "An army never goes to battle without a second line of defense."

Since we were dealing with a life-and-death situation and Craig's healing hadn't instantly manifested, we believed God was leading us to adopt a "second line of defense." We decided to let the doctors perform surgery to remove the tumor.

We were still standing in faith for Craig's healing, but at that point we began to focus our prayers on the operation ahead. We prayed for God to guide the surgeon's hands, and we also put our faith out for this tumor to be benign and not malignant. Above all, we prayed that the doctors would be able to remove the tumor without any damage or negative side effects.

One of the most miraculous things about this whole situation was that this tumor should have affected Craig's coordination, but it didn't. He passed every coordination test the doctors gave him. I'm so thankful that God can keep us and preserve us, even in the middle of the devil's attack.

As we prepared for the surgery, I was at home packing so I could stay with Craig while he was in the hospital. As I stood there in the middle of my closet, I began to cry out to the Lord, "God, I need to feel You right now! I know we walk by faith, but I need to feel Your Presence. I need to hear Your voice. I need You to speak to me!"

Really, I just needed to feel the comfort of the Holy Spirit, reassuring me that everything was going to be okay. I knew it already in my heart, but I needed to feel God's Presence right at that moment because I felt so all alone.

God is so precious to grant our desires! I had barely gotten those words out of my mouth when something dropped from the closet shelf and landed on the floor right in front of me. I wasn't sure what it was, so I stooped down and picked it up.

I discovered it was a small lapel pin that someone had given us a few months earlier, and it had a little saying written on it—"You can make it!"

I'll tell you what—the words on that pin were like God speaking directly to me in an audible voice. He was saying, "Lynette, you can make it!"

"Thank You, God," I sighed with relief. "I'm going to use this pin to minister to my son!"

I was so excited as I rushed upstairs to Craig's bedroom and told him, "Son, look! The Lord has just dropped a pin from Heaven. This pin says, 'You can make it!' We're going to pin this on you, and if fear tries to grip you when you go into that operating room, just remember that the pin says, 'You can make it!'"

It was amazing how God confirmed what He had spoken to us through that little pin! When the doctors performed surgery on our son, he was in the operating room for 12 hours—the longest 12 hours of our lives. But no matter how long we sat in that waiting room, I had confidence in the Lord that Craig was going to make it.

When the medical team came out of the operating room, they told us, "This was a textbook surgery."

"What does that mean?" we asked them.

"No instrument was dropped," they replied. "Nothing—absolutely nothing—went wrong."

Not only was this a "textbook surgery," but one of the nurses who assisted the anesthesiologist was a long-time partner of our ministry. She had been standing in faith for a healing from a chronic back condition, and the power of God was so strong during Craig's surgery that she was completely healed in that operating room!

The doctors told us afterward that they were unable to remove the little lip edge of the tumor, so we agreed in prayer that this remnant would completely disappear. Later, when we took Craig back to the hospital for a checkup, every trace of that tumor had vanished!

Today Craig is perfectly healthy, with no negative side effects from the tumor or the surgery. He's a grown man now—a college graduate with three children of his own—and he also works full-time with us in the ministry. Thank God, the Lord has completely restored him from the devil's attack!

I don't know what crisis has come your way or what fiery trial you may be experiencing right now. But I know that the same God Who met me in the middle of my fiery trial will meet you in the middle of yours. And He's going to cause you to triumph over it, just as He promised in His Word (2 Cor. 2:14).

Don't Be Shocked When the Fire Gets Hot

The Apostle Peter said something in First Peter 4:12 about the fiery trials of life that really grabbed my attention. He said, *"Don't be surprised at the fiery trials you are going through, as if something strange were happening to you"* (NLT).

In other words, Peter warned us not to be shocked when the flames of the fire are roaring all around us. He also said in First Peter 1:7 that the trial of our faith is ". . . *much more precious than of gold that perisheth, though it be tried with fire. . . .*"

God wants us to know that the fiery trials of life will come. Our faith will be tested by going through the fire. But the Lord also said in Isaiah 43:2, ". . . *When thou walkest through the fire, thou shalt not be burned; neither shall the flame kindle upon thee.*" That's a promise we can stand on when we're going through the fiery trials of life.

I'll never forget one time when Ken and I visited a gold mine in South Africa and we watched the process involved in refining gold. You see, gold has impurities in it, and before it can be used for jewelry or coins or any other purpose, the impurities must be burned out.

Ken and I watched in amazement as gold from that mine was placed in a big crucible, thrust into the fire, and heated until it melted. As the fire burned, you could see the impurities rising to the top. Then they were skimmed off so the gold could be used for whatever purpose was desired.

In the same way, you and I may feel as if we're roasting in the middle of a great, big fire. But when we see the impurities rising to the top, we need to remember that God wants those things to be skimmed off and purged out of our lives.

Now let's be real about this for a moment. The fiery trials and testings of our faith aren't much fun, are they?

Sometimes when the tests come, I tell the Lord, "God, this isn't worth it. It's too hard. I want to give up!"

But each time those thoughts come, the Greater One on the inside of me rises up and I begin to say, "Yes, I'm being tested by the fire, but I'm also being purified. And I'm determined that I will come out of the fire like pure gold."

In Daniel chapter 3, we read that Shadrach, Meshach, and Abednego were tried in the fire. But I want you to notice that they weren't thrown into the flames because they did anything wrong. They were cast into King Nebuchadnezzar's burning, fiery furnace because they did something right—because they refused to bow down to the king's golden image.

The three Hebrew children declared, *"Our God, whom we serve, is able to deliver us . . . and He WILL deliver us . . ."* (v. 17). That was their faith talking. But they added to that a statement of their commitment to the Lord. They said, "But even if God doesn't deliver us, we will not serve your gods or worship the golden image that you have set up" (v. 18).

When we go through a fiery trial of life, it's so important for us to have faith. But we also need to have a commitment to the Lord such as the three Hebrew children had. We need to be committed, as Job was when he said, *"Though he [God] slay me, yet will I trust in him . . ."* (Job 13:15).

Yes, the three Hebrew children were cast into the burning, fiery furnace, but the Lord Jesus Christ met them in the middle of the fire. They had to go through the fire, but when they came out, they didn't smell like smoke. Their hair wasn't singed. Their clothes weren't burned. There weren't any signs that they had ever *been* in the fire.

And when they came out of the furnace, they were singing the praises of their God! Not only that, but the king was praising God too. He issued a decree that if anybody said anything bad about the God of Shadrach, Meshach, and Abednego, they would be put to death, " '. . . *because there is no other god that can deliver like this*' " (Daniel 3:29 NKJV).

We're all going to be tested by the fire. Why? Because Satan is the god of this world, and he is our adversary. First Peter 5:8 says that he goes about as a roaring lion, seeking whom he may devour. But he can't devour us if we won't allow it.

You may feel as if you've been in the fire so long that you're already burned to a crisp. You may feel that you can't make it through one more test or trial of life. But you can—because Philippians 4:13 says, "*I can do all things through Christ who strengthens me*" (NKJV).

Count It All Joy

Have you ever thought your faith was well-developed in a certain area, but when it came time to act on God's Word, you found out that your faith wasn't as strong as you thought it was? Do you know why that happened? The revelation of the Word wasn't really down inside your heart.

When that happens, you have to go back and meditate on the Word some more until it gets down deep into your spirit—until it's *real* to you.

No matter how much we meditate on and believe the Word, our faith will never grow without trying and testing. Yes, faith *comes* by hearing, and hearing by the Word of God (Rom. 10:17). But faith *grows* as it's tested. And it won't be tested just once. There will be many tests and trials of our faith.

James 1:2 says, "*Count it all joy when you fall into divers temptations.*" The *New International Version* says, "*Consider it pure joy, my brothers, whenever you face trials of many kinds. . . .*" Why? "*. . . because you know that the testing of your faith develops perseverance*" (v. 3).

You can rejoice when the tests and trials of life come, because it's the testing time that builds your endurance. And if that doesn't make you feel like shouting, then you can rejoice because God said the trial of your faith is going to cause you to come forth like pure gold—it's going to make you shine (1 Peter 1:7).

The Apostle Paul knew what it was like to be tested by fire. Second Corinthians 11:24–28 says that he was beaten five times with 39 stripes and three times with rods. Once he was stoned and three times he suffered shipwreck. For a day and a night he was tossed about in the deep.

He was in perils in the city, perils in the wilderness, perils in the sea, and perils among false brethren. Paul was in perils all the time! Can you identify with him?

He said, ". . . *In weariness and painfulness, in watchings often, in hunger and thirst . . .*" (v. 27). That means he didn't even have the money to satisfy his hunger. Paul had more afflictions, trials, and troubles than anyone I know of, but he was still able to boldly say, "*Thanks be unto God, which always causeth us to triumph in Christ . . .*" (2 Cor. 2:14). And because Paul could say that, we are able to boldly proclaim it too.

The next time the fire gets hot and the devil starts howling in your ear, let those words of the Apostle Paul ring over and over in your heart. Just begin to declare, as he did, "Now thanks be unto God, Who *always* causes me to triumph in my Lord and Savior, Jesus Christ!"

CHAPTER 7

CLIMBING OUT FROM UNDER A DARK CLOUD

One day my best friend, Lanell, called me at work because she was having a terrible day. She was feeling down and discouraged, and as soon as I answered the phone, she blurted out, "Do you like me?"

I thought to myself, *What planet is she coming from?* But then I said, "Of course I like you. Why?"

"Oh, I'm just having some problems today. I feel like nobody likes me, and I had to talk to somebody who likes me."

"Yes, I like you," I assured her, and then I added, "I want to tell you a funny story." So I began to tell Lanell one funny story after the other until she finally burst out laughing.

After a few minutes, she said to me, "I really needed to laugh today!"

Sometimes we all need a good laugh to cheer us up and get us out of the depressing moods that try to come against us. Proverbs 17:22 says, "*A merry heart does good, like medicine, But a broken spirit dries the bones*" (NKJV). I want to tell you a story that illustrates what that scripture is talking about here.

All of my life I was extremely close to my father. I was definitely a "daddy's girl." In fact, I was my dad's favorite child. (But don't tell my sister and brother!)

One of the most devastating times I have ever been through in my life was when my precious daddy passed away. Even though he was 89 years old, almost 90, I still wasn't ready for him to go home to be with the Lord. It was like cutting my earthly umbilical cord, and it hurt.

I'll never forget the Sunday after Dad's memorial service. My husband and I had gone to church that morning, but somehow I hadn't received the touch I needed from the Lord. When we got back to the hotel where we were staying, a horrible feeling of depression started to close in on me.

Instantly I recognized what it was, and I knew I had to do something about it. So I turned on the television, hoping to find something uplifting to watch, but I couldn't find any Christian TV stations. As I flipped through the channels, I kept thinking, *Lord, I need to hear something that lifts my spirits. I'm sinking deeper and deeper, and I need Your help!*

All at once, I saw Art Linkletter's face flash across the TV screen, and I remembered how much I had always enjoyed watching his TV programs, *People Are Funny* and *Kids Say the Darndest Things*. I admired him very much so I began listening to what he was saying. Actually, he was celebrating his 90th birthday, and he looked wonderful.

All of a sudden, he began to describe what had helped him to be a success through the years. He said, "I've never stopped learning. I'm always looking for something new to learn. And I've always kept laughter in my heart."

By the time I finished listening to Art Linkletter that day, I was laughing and my spirits were lifted too.

Now that program wasn't exactly the kind of encouragement I expected to receive from the Lord. But it just proves that God is not limited in what He can use to cheer us up and encourage our hearts.

That's why it's so important for us to always be looking for even the tiniest things God may send our way to encourage us. We need to reach out and receive every possible form of encouragement we can from the Lord.

I Didn't Want to Smile Ever Again

I remember another time when God used one of the most unusual things to lift my spirits—the church service announcements! It's been my experience that announcement time is one of the driest parts of most church services. But God can use even a dry announcement time to bless and lift our spirits.

This incident happened during a Wednesday night service several years ago when I did *not* feel like going to church. Yes, I'm human just like you are. I'm not always thrilled about going to church. At times, I would rather stay home. But I know if I do, I might miss the help I so desperately need from the Lord.

This particular Wednesday night I was extremely tired and upset. I had been confronted with a lot of difficult situations that week, and I was hurting. To be perfectly honest, I was at the point of tears.

I didn't want to smile ever again. I didn't want to say "Hi" to anyone. And I certainly didn't want to act as if I was on top of the world when I felt I was sinking below the bottom. I was so frustrated and upset that I really wanted to crawl in a hole and say, "Forget this!"

But it was Wednesday night, and I was the pastor's wife. I was expected to go to church. So I went to church with my husband as usual, and I didn't tell a soul, including him, how badly I felt.

As the service began, I was just sitting there, praying silently, "God, I need something from You. Please help me, Lord." It was so amazing how the Lord began to minister to me from the very beginning of the service. It seemed as if every worship song spoke to me in a special way, and as I began to worship the Lord, my spirit was lifted dramatically.

Then one of our associate pastors began to give the announcements. Suddenly, in the middle of the announcements, he began to minister by the Holy Spirit. He spoke words of prophecy and comfort, and those were exactly the right words for me.

As he spoke, I thought, *Oh my goodness! How did he get inside my head? He doesn't even know what I'm going through!* But the Holy Spirit knew. And the words the Holy Spirit prompted him to say ministered so much life and encouragement to me.

Next my husband got up to preach, and even though I hadn't told him what kind of day I was having, he began to minister to my needs very powerfully. As he preached that night, the words that came out of his mouth were coming *through* him but they were not *from* him. His words were coming straight from the Spirit of God to my heart. His message ministered to me so much that by the end of the service, instead of being depressed, I was having a shouting-good time!

When I went to the service that night, I was below the bottom of the barrel. But as I reached out to the Lord in faith, He ministered to me through every possible avenue. It's so important for us to be open to the Lord and receive His encouragement in whatever way He wants to give it!

The Praise Cure

I remember another situation that took place in our ministry several years ago when one of our departments had somehow gotten off track. The whole department seemed to be in chaos, and it was very depressing. As I worked to get things back in proper order, I could feel a cloud of depression trying to come over me.

I told some of my staff members, "Please get me some music tapes! I need to listen to some joyful, upbeat music. I don't want to hear any slow songs. I need to hear some lively praise music to help get my spirits back up again."

So we started bringing music tapes to work with us, and all day long we played uplifting praise music for the employees in that department. I also encouraged them, saying, "We're not going to get depressed. We're going to get ourselves back on the right course *with joy!*" And we did!

You see, it is important that we reach our divine destination in life. But it is just as important that we reach that destination with joy! The Apostle Paul said in Acts 20:24, "*None of these things move me . . . so that I might finish my course with joy . . . .*" If it was important to Paul to finish his course with joy, it should be important to us too.

Isaiah 61:3 tells us that God has given us a "praise cure" to help us overcome the depression and discouragement that try to come against all of us in this life. He's given us ". . . *the garment of praise for the spirit of heaviness. . . .*" The Lord is saying to us, "Praise Me and worship Me during those dark and troubled times, and I will set you free."

If you want to rise above the dark clouds of depression and discouragement, surround yourself with music that ministers to you, personally. There's nothing like praise music that speaks directly to your heart.

When Satan attacks you with discouragement and depression, begin to give praise to God. Surround yourself with uplifting, upbeat praise music. Tell the Lord how much you appreciate Him. Just say to Him, "Father, I love You. I thank You for all that You've done for me." And remember that the Lord inhabits the praises of His people (Ps. 22:3).

As human beings, we respond to the praises of our children, don't we? I mean, when that little girl crawls up in daddy's lap and puts her arms around him and says, "I love you so much, Daddy. You're so wonderful to me. You're such a great daddy!" his heart just melts. And when she gets to the point of asking him for something, the answer usually is, "Oh, honey, whatever you want." And he gives her even more than she asks for.

When we praise our Heavenly Father, He opens His arms to us and says, "Oh, child, you can have whatever you want. Is that all you want? I have so much more for you!" Then He surrounds us with His presence, and that's when the clouds begin to lift, because in His presence there is fullness of joy (Ps. 16:11). Those old dark clouds of depression and discouragement can't stay in the presence of our God!

Confirmation From the Lord in a Small Town

Not long after my dad passed away, my father-in-law also went home to be with the Lord, totally unexpectedly. All at once, my husband and I had both lost our natural, earthly fathers. We had lost the people who had mentored us all of our lives. And when Brother Hagin went home to be with the Lord, we had also lost our business partner.

It was a very difficult time for us and we were so thankful for the comforting power of the Holy Spirit. But suddenly we were thrust into a new position in life. We thought we had been busy before. All at once we went into overdrive!

We were already responsible for the administration of the ministry, so nothing changed in that area. But Brother Hagin had always been there to give us the vision he wanted us to accomplish. After his death, the entire direction of the ministry was suddenly on our shoulders. Listening to your head at a time like that can be mind-boggling!

Instead, we looked to the Holy Ghost for help—for His comfort, His wisdom, His guidance and direction. We drew upon the strengthening power of the Holy Spirit, and He was there for us every step of the way.

But after a few months, our bodies grew extremely weary. We had been going at such a horrendous pace that we decided to take a little vacation.

When we go on vacation, we like to visit all the small, rural towns—the towns where hardly anyone ever recognizes us from our TV programs or public ministry. We just wanted to have a little "hibernation" time and get some rest.

When your body is weary, that's when the Enemy loves to talk to your mind. He always comes to you at your weakest moments, just as he came to Jesus and tempted

Him when He was weak with hunger in the wilderness (see Luke 4:1–13).

So the Enemy was whispering in our ears during our vacation and trying to discourage us, trying to make us think that all of our hard work was a waste of time. You know how he talks to you. Well, he talks to us the same way.

After a day or two, I began to feel depression and darkness trying to come over me, so I asked my Heavenly Father for some encouragement. I said, "God, I just need a little confirmation right now. I know that what we're doing is worth it. I really do. But I need to hear it from someone here on this earth." Remember, when you ask your Heavenly Father for something in faith, for something that's in line with His Word, He will give it to you.

So there we were in this little rural town. We went to what seemed to be the only restaurant. Just as we sat down to eat, a man came up to us and introduced himself. He said, "You don't know me, but I know you. I just listened to your radio program this morning, and you ministered to my heart. You lifted me up. I was discouraged, and your words completely changed my life!"

God used that man's words to answer my heart's cry and give both of us some much-needed encouragement. Our spirits were immediately lifted, and we went on our way praising God!

The next day we went to another little Oklahoma town, trusting that nobody there would know us. Remember, we were hiding! We decided to go to one of our favorite discount stores. We were in the sporting goods department, just looking around, when this man walked by us. Then he turned around and walked by us again. After a few moments, he asked my husband, "Who are you?"

"I'm Kenneth Hagin."

"I thought that was you," the man continued. "I watch you on television every week. My, what a blessing you have been in my life!"

That was confirmation number two. Hallelujah! God will do exceedingly abundantly above all that we can ask or think (Eph. 3:20). And that man's words lifted our spirits just a little bit more.

The next day, we were in another little town, sitting down to eat one of our favorite meals—catfish. We were just minding our own business, eating our meal, when a man came over to us and said the famous line—"You don't know me, but I know you."

Then he went on to say, "Several years ago, when your daughter was a student at Oklahoma State University, my son was in charge of a campus ministry there. You and your daughter came to visit their campus house one night, and God laid it on your heart to help them fix up their house. It needed a whole lot of fixing, so you gave them several thousand dollars to help.

"You don't know what a blessing that was to my son. He was getting so discouraged that he was just about to quit. He was even beginning to wonder if God still loved him. When you ministered to him through that gift, it completely changed his life. Now he's pastoring a church and doing mighty things for the Lord."

Praise God, that was confirmation number three! By this time, our hearts were rejoicing and the depression that had been trying to creep in on us was far, far away.

Don't Camp in the Valley

Have you ever experienced depression? If you have, then you know how the dark clouds can come rolling in on you. Everything around you starts getting darker and darker, and if you allow yourself to be engulfed in that darkness, it will totally surround you. But thank God, the Lord has made a way for you to climb out from under those dark clouds.

If you're feeling down and discouraged, if you feel like it's just not worth it, call on the Lord and He will give you the confirmation and encouragement you need. Start praising Him and listening to praise music, and you will feel your spirit lifted. And always make room for laughter in your life.

Yes, you may walk through the valley, but you're not supposed to camp there. You're supposed to cross over to the other side.

On the other side there is joy, peace, and an assignment from the Lord. Just ask Him to let that assignment burn so brightly in your heart that it will light your path all the way to victory!

CHAPTER 8

THE
SOMETHING-FOR-JESUS-TO-DO
BOX

Several years ago, my husband and I had reached the stage in our lives where our children were grown, and all at once, we were facing the "empty-nest syndrome." For years, we had done all kinds of activities with our kids. But we suddenly realized that we needed to find something *we* liked to do, just the two of us.

I knew that any activity we became involved in would probably have to relate to sports, because, next to preaching, sports is my husband's favorite activity. But sports is my worst talent!

Really, I believe God must have a sense of humor when He puts a man who is very athletic with a woman who doesn't have an athletic bone in her body. I mean, if you throw a ball at me, I'm going to try to catch it with my eyes closed! So I began to wonder, *What on earth can we learn to do together?*

Finally, we decided we would try fishing. Of course, I couldn't stand *to bait* a hook, much less take a fish off the hook. But I do like the water. So my husband agreed to bait my hook and take any fish I caught off the hook. And I thought, *Okay, we'll try fishing!*

At first we went crappie fishing. That was easy because you don't have to cast your line if you want to catch crappie. You just put your pole into the water and the crappie will hit your line. I thought that was wonderful and so exciting—at least for a little while.

Then we saw some plaques with these great, big fish mounted on them, and we began to think, *Wouldn't it be fun to catch some of the big fish?* But you don't catch big fish without learning how to cast.

We had seen several fishing programs on television and the fishermen made casting look so easy. We tried desperately to imitate what we had seen them do, but in spite of our best efforts, we weren't catching any fish. Instead, we usually wound up snagging each other's hair with our fishhooks.

We were wild with our casting! We were catching each other's bodies, not fish! To be honest, we were taking our lives in our hands. But we kept on practicing.

We would cast the line out a few feet and then reel it back in. Then we would cast out a little farther and reel the line back in again. Just because we had fishing poles in our hands didn't mean we could automatically cast well. It took practice for us to learn. And with a whole lot of practice, we were finally able to catch those big fish.

Start Casting the Little Things First

Did you know that God has some "casting" He wants us to do, spiritually speaking? First Peter 5:7 says, *"Casting all your care upon Him* [God], *for He cares for you"* (NKJV). *The Amplified Bible* says, *"Casting the whole of your care [all your anxieties, all your worries, all your concerns, once and for all] on Him, for He cares for you affectionately and cares about you watchfully."* To live a worry-free life and escape the hurt and damage that stress can cause, we must learn how to cast our cares on the Lord.

I want you to think for just a moment about what you would do if you received a telephone call from the Lord one morning. Imagine answering the phone and saying, "Good morning," and then hearing on the other end of the line, "This is God. Today I will be handling all of your problems. Please remember that I do not need your help in doing so. If the devil happens to deliver a situation to you that you cannot handle, do not attempt to resolve it.

"Kindly put it in the SFJTD (Something-for-Jesus-to-Do) Box. Once the matter is placed in the box, do not hold on to it or attempt to remove it. Holding on or removing will delay the resolution of your problem.

"If it's a situation that you think you're capable of handling, please consult Me in prayer to be sure that you've chosen the proper resolution. Remember, I do not sleep, nor do I slumber. That means there's no need for *you* to lose any sleep.

So rest, My child. If you need to contact Me, I am only a prayer away."

The author of that inspirational message is unknown, but I'm sure if you were to get that kind of phone call from the Lord, it would startle you. Well, you're getting that kind of "call" from the Lord every day through His Word! He's saying to you every morning, "Cast all of your cares on Me."

Casting your cares on the Lord is a lot like casting a fishing line. The first time you try it may turn out to be a catastrophe. You may feel as if you're getting the fishhooks caught in your hair. But you have to keep practicing. You have to keep casting your cares on the Lord.

As I said, when my husband and I started learning how to fish, we only caught the little fish at first. You may need to start by casting the little things on the Lord at first. For example, maybe you've been worrying about everything. But instead of trying to cast every single care on the Lord, why don't you pick just one of the little things that you've been upset about and start by casting it on the Lord? Start with one worry at a time, and practice your casting. After you learn how to cast the little things on the Lord, then you can go on to the bigger things.

Why is it important for you to cast your cares on the Lord? Because if you don't, your mind is going to be so cluttered with worries and stress that it will be hard for you to fulfill God's plan for your life. Besides, the Lord loves you so much that He doesn't want you to be weighed down by those burdens. First Corinthians 7:32 in *The Amplified Bible* says that He wants you to be free "... *from all anxiety and distressing care*"!

You Don't Have to Play by the Devil's Rules

After you start casting your cares on the Lord as it says in First Peter 5:7, that doesn't mean the devil is going to automatically stop harassing you. The very next verse says, *"Be sober, be vigilant; because your adversary the devil, as a roaring lion, walketh about, seeking whom he may devour."*

When you cast your cares on the Lord, don't be surprised if the Enemy immediately tries to challenge you. For example, if you begin to declare by faith, "I cast the care of my finances on the Lord," in the next instant, the devil is probably going to remind you, "You don't have enough money to pay all of those bills that are due."

But you have to keep casting. You can declare by faith, "God's Word says that He will supply all of my need according to His riches in glory by Christ Jesus (Phil. 4:19). My Father owns the cattle on a thousand hills, and that wealth is mine too (Ps. 50:10)."

Or if your job is being eliminated and the Enemy taunts you by saying, "What are you going to do now?" just cast that care on the Lord. You can boldly declare, "My Heavenly Father is Jehovah Jireh. He's my Provider, and He's going to take care of me!"

Or suppose you cast your cares and worries about your health on the Lord. Don't be surprised if the Enemy suddenly starts yelling in your ear, "Who are you kidding? You're not healed. Your body is racked with pain, and just look at your symptoms."

But you have to keep on casting. Declare by faith, "Mr. Devil, I'm casting my cares on the Lord because His Word says that by the stripes of Jesus I am healed (1 Peter 2:24)."

Yes, Satan will try to keep you filled with worries and cares. But even though you're in the game of life, it doesn't mean you have to play by the devil's rules. You can choose to play by God's rules. And what do God's rules say? Cast your cares on the Lord.

'Now It's Your Problem, Lord'

One of my favorite scriptures in *The Amplified Bible* is Philippians 4:6. It says, "*Do not fret or have any anxiety about anything, but in every circumstance and in everything, by prayer and petition (definite requests), with thanksgiving, continue to make your wants known to God.*"

When the Enemy yells in my ear and tries to get me distracted and worried about a problem or situation, do you know how I keep my sanity? I go to my Heavenly Father, Who gives me the inspiration I need to overcome the devil's attacks. I talk to my Father about the things that are bothering me. And whatever you need, whatever your concerns are, you can talk to the Lord too. He will always be there for you.

I remember when our daughter, Denise, had her first baby. I was at the hospital, trying to help her pack her clothes to come home. All of a sudden, she exclaimed, "Where are the clothes I was wearing when I came to the hospital?"

"I don't know, darling," I replied. "I didn't get here until you were already in a hospital gown."

So she looked over at her husband, Don, and he just shrugged his shoulders and said, "I put them in a bag, but I don't remember where I put the bag. I was so excited about the baby that I have no idea where those clothes went."

I had taken Denise's belongings out of the Labor and Delivery Room, but I didn't realize that the bag with the clothes she had worn to the hospital had been placed somewhere in that room.

Of course, this was two days later, and we were in a very busy hospital. To be perfectly honest, those clothes were lost.

Denise was so concerned about this situation because the slacks she had on when she came to the hospital were the best ones she had. And the missing shoes were the *only* ones she could wear, since her feet were so swollen from her pregnancy.

Naturally, being a new mother, she was a little bit on edge emotionally. She was on the verge of tears as she sighed, "I don't know what I'm going to do. I don't have any shoes to wear home from the hospital."

So Don told her, "I'll go back to Labor and Delivery and see if I can find your clothes."

When he asked the nurse there about Denise's belongings, she halfheartedly checked the room but didn't find anything. Don persisted in trying to find Denise's things, and the nurse began to get aggravated with him.

Finally she told him, "Those clothes are probably down in Housekeeping, and everybody is gone for the weekend. We'll just have to wait until next week to find them."

By the time Denise heard that news, tears had begun to well up in her eyes. So I thought, *I really need to pray about this.*

I whispered very quietly, "Father, we need these clothes, especially these shoes. If they're important to my daughter, they're important to You. You know where they are, and I just thank You for finding them for us."

Then I told Denise, "It's going to be okay. We're going to find those clothes."

Not three minutes later, the same nurse who had said that the clothes were probably in Housekeeping burst into Denise's room, tugging a big white plastic bag behind her. She was so excited as she blurted out, "Here are your clothes!"

I thanked her for helping us and then I said to Denise, "Hallelujah, praise God!"

Instead of worrying about those clothes as I was tempted to do, I did what Philippians 4:6 tells us to do. I made my request known to my Heavenly Father, and then I thanked Him in faith for finding those clothes for us.

Of course, I have faced other situations where I couldn't seem to cast a certain problem over on the Lord, no matter how hard I tried. I remember a few years ago when I was so upset about some things I had been praying about that I started trying to carry that burden myself. In fact, I began to worry about that situation so much that I became completely distraught over it.

Oh, I tried not to worry. I would cast that problem over on the Lord, but almost immediately the devil would drag it back up and throw it in my face. Then I would cast it back over on my Heavenly Father.

Finally, I said to the Lord, "God, You said in Your Word that Your yoke is easy and Your burden is light (Matt. 11:30). This yoke doesn't seem to be easy or this burden light. But You also said that I could give my burdens to You. So I'm giving this problem to You right now by faith."

Then I added, "Now it's Your problem, Lord, and not mine. I'm not going to worry about it anymore because I'm casting my cares on You."

The Lord said to me about that experience, "This is a mere distraction of the devil to keep you from doing what I have called you to do."

Don't let the devil distract you from your calling, your destiny. God has a divine plan for your life and He doesn't want you to be distracted by worry, stress, or anxiety.

Are Your Thoughts Pushing You Around?

In the journey of life, one of the hardest pieces of luggage to shed is worry. It's a tough habit to break. I remember how one little girl explained worry. She described why she was happy one day and unhappy another by saying, "Today I push my thoughts around, and the other day I let my thoughts push *me* around."

So many thoughts and concerns push us around every day. We don't verbalize them, because we're faith people. Why would we want to confess those worries and cares?

But stress and worry have become a way of life for so many of us. Sometimes we think we're not worrying about something, but it may be dogging us on the inside.

Those worries are filling us with anxiety, and yet the Lord, Who loves us so much, is saying to us, "Give them to Me, child! Cast those worries, cares, and all of that stress on Me." God wants us to stop wringing our hands and start doing some casting. He wants us to trust Him and let Him handle all the cares of life for us.

If you've been concerned about anything at all, I want you to cast that burden over on the Lord by faith right now. You may have financial cares and worries. It's important that you do all you can about your financial situation, but then you have to cast the rest on the Lord.

Or maybe you have family problems. After you've done what you can about those problems, cast them on your Heavenly Father. And as you do, declare by faith, "Once and for all, I'm casting this situation on my God!"

I believe that as you cast those burdens, cares, and worries on the Lord, you're going to feel your load grow lighter. You're going to rise to a new level—a level where you've never been before.

All of that stress and worry has been dragging you down. But as you cast it on your Heavenly Father, He will lift you up and carry you through the trials and hard places. And you will come out on the other side of every problem, rejoicing in the Lord!

CHAPTER 9

THE MIND—A POWERFUL ALLY OR AN AWESOME ENEMY

I refuse to think of myself as being "old," even though I'm certainly older now than I used to be. I praise the Lord that I'm naturally endowed with a lot of energy. As a result, my friends and family often call me the "Energizer Bunny." To be honest, most people have to run to keep up with me.

A few years ago, I turned the big 6-0. I've never dreaded a birthday before in my life. I flew through 40—that birthday didn't even bother me. Turning 50 didn't bother me either. But when I started creeping up on 57, 58, and then 59—oh my! I clung to 59 for dear life!

I used to tease my husband about his age (he's six years older than I am). When he was 37, I would laugh and tell him, "You're only 3 years away from 40." I loved to taunt him and I thought it was so funny.

But when I started nearing 60, I stopped teasing my husband about his age. All of a sudden, I began to understand how he must have felt when I teased him all of those years. And the closer I got to 60, the more tempted I was to be a little bit depressed about my age. To me, 60 sounded so old.

On the other hand, I reminded myself, *No! This is not the end. It's just the beginning!* Even though the years were obviously ticking away, I realized that what I focused my mind and thoughts on was going to determine what I was able to accomplish during the rest of my life.

You see, Proverbs 23:7 tells us, "*As* [a man] *thinketh in his heart, so is he.*" That means if I start thinking "old," I'm going to be old. So I've decided not to focus on being a certain age. Instead, I'm going to focus on what God says about me in His Word.

For example, I'm going to focus on Romans 8:11 that says, "The same Spirit that raised Christ from the dead dwells in me and quickens my mortal body." I'm going to focus on Psalm 103:5 that says, "He satisfies my mouth with good things so that my youth is renewed like the eagle's."

Every year as I get older, I'm going to program myself to think younger. Why? Because according to Proverbs 23:7, it's how we think that's important. So I'm declaring by faith that I'm still going to be young when I reach 95, and I'm going to accomplish everything God wants me to accomplish.

I encourage you today, don't start thinking "old"—ever. Remember, your mind can be either a powerful ally or an awesome enemy. Your thoughts can make you victorious in life or they can utterly defeat you.

You cannot think thoughts of defeat and expect to receive victory. You cannot think thoughts of sickness and expect to receive health. You cannot think thoughts of poverty and expect to receive prosperity.

Refuse to think the negative thoughts and the lies that Satan has told you. Remember, your mind is the bull's eye on the devil's target. He's constantly bombarding your mind with negative ideas and images. He will dog you with thoughts of gloom, doom, and defeat as long as you allow him to get by with it. But you don't have to let the devil dominate your thought life.

Instead of letting Satan program your mind to think defeated thoughts, you can program your mind to think victorious thoughts. Start thinking about yourself the way God thinks about you—the way His Word says you are. If you choose to think these kinds of thoughts, you will live a victorious life.

What Are You Focusing On?

It's so easy for us to focus our thoughts on the problems that are threatening to overwhelm us, but the Bible is filled with encouraging words to help us focus on God and His mighty delivering power. Psalm 91:15 says, *"He shall call upon me, and I* [God] *will answer him: I will be with him in trouble; I will deliver him, and honour him."*

Did you notice that the Lord said, *"I will deliver him"*? That's a wonderful promise of God's deliverance for your life and mine.

Romans 8:35,37 says, *"Who shall separate us from the love of Christ? shall tribulation, or distress, or persecution, or famine, or nakedness, or peril, or sword? . . . Nay, in all these things we are more than conquerors through him that loved us."* Notice that it says we're not just "conquerors." It says we're "more than conquerors"! These verses can help us think victorious thoughts.

A story in John chapter 6 describes how some of Jesus' ministry employees were having trouble keeping their thoughts focused on God's delivering power. Instead, all they could think about was the problem staring them in the face. Let's look at that story in *The Amplified Bible.*

A huge crowd of people was following Jesus one day. It was getting late and the people were hungry. So the Lord asked His disciples, *"Where are we to buy bread, so that all these people may eat?"* (v. 5).

Of course, the disciples were shocked by His question. Philip exclaimed, *"Two hundred pennies' (forty dollars) worth of bread is not enough that everyone may receive even a little"* (v. 7).

Then Andrew told the Lord, *"There is a little boy here, who has . . . five barley loaves, and two small fish. . . ."* However, his faith immediately began to waver as he added, *". . . But what are they among so many people?"* (v. 9).

Notice that the disciples focused on their lack, on what they did not have. If it had been left up to them, that great crowd of people would have gone hungry.

But Jesus focused on what they did have. He told Andrew to bring the five loaves and two little fish to Him. Then the Lord multiplied the loaves and fishes and fed five thousand men plus all the women and children who were there.

I believe God is saying to us through this story, "Refuse to focus on what you don't have. Instead, focus on what you do have. Focus on Me and My delivering power, and I will multiply what you have into a wonderful miracle."

But in order for that to happen, we have to keep our minds fixed and focused on the Lord, Who is our Deliverer. Satan will try to get our minds off-track and focused on the problem. But when our minds are focused on God and His Word, that's when miracles happen!

My Mind Is Giving Me Fits

We all have trouble sometimes focusing on the right things, but thank God, the Bible tells us exactly what to focus our thoughts on. Isaiah 26:3 says, "*Thou wilt keep him in perfect peace, whose mind is stayed* [or focused] *on thee: because he trusteth in thee.*" Let's read that verse in *The Amplified Bible*: "*You will guard him and keep him in perfect and constant peace whose mind [both its inclination and its character] is stayed on You, because he commits himself to You, leans on You, and hopes confidently in You.*"

Let me ask you, have you totally committed yourself to the Lord? Do you lean on Him and hope confidently in Him?

I lean on the Lord on a daily basis. When I wake up in the morning, I say to Him, "These are the decisions I must make today. I don't have the answers, but You said in Your Word that if any man lacks wisdom, let him ask of You, and You will give it to him liberally (James 1:5). Thank You for giving me the wisdom to make the right decisions today." And God always gives me the wisdom I need.

If you'll lean on the Lord, He'll give you strength and wisdom too. He will keep you in perfect peace, according to Isaiah 26:3!

The problem with most of us is that we're trying to live a peaceful and victorious life without keeping our minds focused on the Lord. To enjoy the peace our Heavenly Father wants us to have, we must keep our minds fixed and focused on Him.

Another wonderful scripture, Philippians 4:8, tells us what God wants us to think about. Let's read this verse from *The Living Bible*: "*. . . Fix your thoughts on what is true and good and right. Think about things that are pure and lovely, and dwell on the fine, good things in others.*"

The *King James Version* puts it this way: "*Finally, brethren, whatsoever things are true, whatsoever things are honest, whatsoever things are just, whatsoever things are pure, whatsoever things are lovely, whatsoever things are of good report; if there be any virtue, and if there be any praise, think on these things.*" Can you imagine how much better our lives would be if we constantly focused our minds and thoughts on these things!

God is telling us in this verse to think about things that will build us up, not tear us down. I encourage you to think about all the wonderful things God has already done for you. Focus on the positive things in life. If you're thinking about the good things of God, you're not going to have time to worry, complain, and get discouraged. If you're continually meditating on God's promises, you're always going to be filled with a good report.

It's Time to Renew Our Minds

Romans 12:2 tells us, *"Do not be conformed to this world, but be transformed by the renewing of your mind . . . "* (NKJV). What does it mean to "renew your mind?" It means to train your mind to think only thoughts that are in line with God's Word. It means to meditate on the Word of God and study the Word until your thoughts "conform to" what His Word says.

When your mind is renewed, if sickness comes knocking on your door and pain is attacking your body, you refuse to react the way the rest of the world normally does. Instead, you immediately begin to think about what God's Word says. You think about the healing covenant you have with the Lord.

Instead of thinking, *Oh, something is terribly wrong with me. I'm probably going to die!* you think about what the Bible says in Matthew 8:17—"Jesus Himself took my infirmities and bore my sicknesses." You think about what God's Word says in First Peter 2:24—"By Jesus' wounds, I was healed." You focus your mind on the Word of God and refuse to focus on the symptoms that are attacking your body.

That doesn't mean you deny the symptoms exist. Faith is not denying the symptoms. Faith declares that the Word of God is more powerful than any symptom!

Is it easy? No. Nobody ever said it would be easy. But the results are certainly worth it. Your life will be dramatically changed if you train your mind to think in line with God's Word.

Do you remember the scripture we talked about at the beginning of this chapter—"*As* [a man] *thinketh in his heart, so is he*" (Prov. 23:7)? If you constantly think of yourself as weak and sickly, you're probably going to be weak and sickly. But if you think of yourself the way God thinks of you—as being healed by the stripes laid on Jesus' back—that's the way you will be, according to God's Word!

If poverty or lack comes knocking on your door, instead of thinking thoughts of failure and devastation, focus your thoughts on what the Bible says. Focus on Psalm 37:25: "... *I have never seen the righteous forsaken or their children begging bread*" (NIV). Think about Philippians 4:19—"*My God shall supply all your need according to his riches in glory by Christ Jesus.*"

The more you renew your mind, the more you'll refuse to meditate on how big your problems are. Instead, you'll meditate and dwell on how big your God is. While the rest of the world worries about what the stock market is doing, you'll be thinking about what God is doing to meet your needs. You'll be rejoicing that He can still rain down manna from Heaven, *because He hasn't lost the recipe*!

Don't Let Studying God's Word Become a Routine or Ritual

If we're going to train our minds to think according to God's Word, we have to study and meditate on the Word and make sure that it's getting down into our hearts. That's why it's important for us not to let studying the Word become a routine or ritual.

Sometimes we find ourselves reading the Bible over and over again, but it's not really getting down into our spirits. As you read God's Word, I encourage you to make sure that you're actually soaking that Word into your heart. If you don't understand things in the Word of God, ask the Lord to illuminate them for you. Ask Him to help you understand what the Bible is saying in those passages.

Brother Hagin told of a man who had faithfully attended several meetings where he taught on faith. After about the 13th meeting, the man came up to him and said, "I got it! I finally got it!" I guess our minds are a little thick sometimes. But there's nothing more precious in this life than receiving the Word of God.

Without God's Word, I don't know where I would be. His Word is what has kept me throughout my life. When trials and tests come, when tribulations come—whatever comes—I can always go to the Word of God.

It seems that many Christians today have trouble sticking with the Word, especially in the tough times. As long as they're prospering and everything is going fine, it's easy for them to confess the Word. But when the tests and trials come, when the "having done all to stand" time comes (Eph. 6:13), they fly away and leave the Word far behind.

It's absolutely vital for us to stand firm on the foundation of God's Word. Isaiah 53:1 (NKJV) asks the question, *"Who has believed our report?"* Our answer should always be, "I believe the report of God's Word."

It takes toughness and tenacity to fight the good fight of faith. It takes staying with the Word of God in the midst of the most devastating problems. So many times we fall short of the blessings God has for us because we don't press in and stay with the Word.

I wonder what would have happened to the woman with the issue of blood if she hadn't been tenacious in her faith and stayed with the Word of God (Mark chapter 5). She had heard about Jesus. She must have heard about the miracles He performed, because she kept saying, "If I can only touch the hem of His garment, I will be made whole." She was sticking with the Word and with her confession of faith.

When this woman set out to touch the hem of Jesus' garment, He was surrounded by a huge crowd. According to Jewish law, she wasn't even supposed to be out in public, because she was considered unclean. I'm sure she must have been trembling with fear, wondering what would happen if someone discovered her condition.

What if she had said, "This is too hard. I'll never make it through this crowd"? What if she had given up and gone home? She wouldn't have received her healing. But she kept pressing through the crowd. She kept her mind focused on Jesus. And she kept speaking out her faith, saying over and over, "If I can only touch the hem of His garment, I will be made whole." She refused to give up, and she was miraculously healed!

It's so important for us to keep pressing on in faith until we receive the answers we're seeking from the Lord and see victory. We must stay focused on the right things—on our Heavenly Father and His Word.

Refuse to Dwell on the Negatives

I remember a story I once read about a man whose business had failed. He went home completely distraught, saying, "I'm ruined! I've lost everything!"

"Everything?" his wife asked him. "I'm still here."

"Papa," his oldest boy said, "I'm here too."

Then his little girl came running up, threw her arms around her father's neck, and whispered, "I'm still here."

His other son said, "I'm here, Papa." And he reminded his father, "Don't forget that you have your health and your hands to work with."

His oldest son added, "And I can help you, Father."

"And you have God's promises," said the grandmother.

"And a good God," said his wife.

"And a Heaven to go to," the little girl chimed in.

All of a sudden, the businessman burst into tears and cried out, "Oh God, forgive me! I haven't lost everything! What have I lost compared with what I have left?"

We have to train ourselves to look at what we have instead of dwelling on what went wrong or what we've lost.

That reminds me of an amazing story I once heard about the great inventor Thomas Edison. It's said that failure never stopped him. He rarely got discouraged when experiments didn't work out. A failed experiment just shifted his thinking in a different direction. That was how he was able to solve problems and learn from his failures. Really, Thomas Edison saw every failure as a success.

The story goes that he failed 10,000 times while working on one of his major inventions. When he was asked about it, he said, "I've just found 10,000 ways that it won't work!" He was focusing on the positive side of the situation instead of the negative side.

It's said that his son recalled a freezing December night in 1914 when the cry of fire echoed through Thomas Edison's plant. It was believed that spontaneous combustion had caused an explosion in one of the buildings, and within minutes its contents had burst into flames.

Fire companies from the surrounding area came to help fight the fire, but the heat was so intense and the water pressure so low that efforts to extinguish the flames were futile. Ten buildings—about half of those in Edison's plant—were destroyed that night, and to make matters worse, Edison's son couldn't find his father. He was especially worried because his father was 67 years old—not an age when most people would think of starting over. He wondered how Edison would handle the situation.

Suddenly, in the distance, young Edison saw his father in the plant yard running toward him, yelling out, "Go get the rest of our family, son! Tell them to bring all of their friends. They'll never see a fire like this again!"

Early the next morning, with the wreckage still too hot to touch, Edison called his employees together and made an incredible announcement. He said, "We're rebuilding. We've just cleared out a bunch of old rubbish. We'll build bigger and better on the ruins." Shortly after that he yawned, rolled up his coat for a pillow, curled up on a table, and immediately fell asleep.

What was Thomas Edison focusing on? Was he dwelling on all the terrible things that had happened and what he had lost? No! He was focusing on the opportunities that were still available to him in the future. And you can do the same thing in your life.

You may have been through something so devastating that it seems like the biggest fire you've ever seen. Disaster may be all around you. But the Lord is saying to you, "Let Me clear out the rubble. I'll help you build something better—on a bigger and better foundation. Let's build something brand new together!"

God has a bigger, better, outrageous, wonderful plan for you. All He has to do is clear out any obstacles that are standing in the way.

Don't focus on the fire anymore. Don't focus on the devastation and loss. Let God clear the rubble out of your life, and then focus on the Lord and His mighty redeeming power.

I encourage you to run to your friends and your family and tell them, "Yes, there's been a fire, but let's see what God will do. Let's see what the miracle power of God can do to bring forth His miraculous plan!"

CHAPTER 10

'HONEY, THIS PLANE SHAKES TOO MUCH!'

I had always struggled with a fear of flying. Every time I boarded an airplane, a terrible spirit of fear tried to grip me. Because we have to frequently travel by air in the ministry, I desperately wanted to get rid of that fear. So I began to search God's Word for scriptures that would help me overcome the fear of flying.

Each time I had to fly somewhere, I read and meditated on those scriptures and quoted them out loud, especially several verses from Psalm 121.

PSALM 121:4-8

4 Behold, he that keepeth Israel shall neither slumber nor sleep.

(I was so thankful that God was not sleeping when I was on that airplane.)

5 The Lord is thy keeper: the Lord is thy shade upon thy right hand.

(Praise God, I knew that the Lord would keep me when I flew on an airplane!)

6 The sun shall not smite thee by day, nor the moon by night.

7 The Lord shall preserve thee from all evil: he shall preserve thy soul.

(The next verse is the one I really claimed.)

8 The Lord shall preserve thy going out and thy coming in from this time forth, and even for evermore.

Every time I was on a plane that was about to lift off the runway, I said, "The Lord will preserve me as I'm going up, and He will preserve me when I'm coming down." Then I faithfully declared the other scriptures that helped me deal with the fear of flying.

Even though I was claiming God's promises to help me overcome my fears, I was still tormented with fearful thoughts every time we had to travel by air. You see, sometimes it takes time for us to build up our faith in a certain area so it's strong enough to drive out fear.

When I first began to confess God's Word to help me overcome the fear of flying, I shook and trembled when we flew through any type of turbulence. One time, I gripped my husband's hand so tightly that it turned red as I whispered to him, "Honey, this plane shakes too much!"

As I continued to meditate on the scriptures concerning fear, I was managing fairly well to fly on the big commercial airliners. I claimed my scriptures right before I boarded a flight and then held tightly to my husband's hand while we were in the air. But anytime we were scheduled to fly on a small, private jet, I could feel that old, panicky feeling rising up in the pit of my stomach again!

One night during a Kenneth Hagin Ministries *Campmeeting*, Brother Hagin was just about to close the service when all of a sudden he said, "Some of you are dealing with fear, and God wants to deliver you this very night."

Now, he didn't have any idea what I was going through, but as soon as he spoke those words, I knew it was my night to be delivered from fear. Immediately, though, I began to wrestle with the thoughts, *Oh God, if I stand up, people will wonder, "What's wrong with her? She's the daughter-in-law of the great man of faith. Why is she dealing with fear?"* Of course, I wasn't too proud to stand up, but all kinds of thoughts were whirling through my mind.

Suddenly, I heard a rustling sound behind me and I peeked around just in time to see a well-known minister stand for prayer. I thought, *God, if he can stand up, I can stand up too. I don't care what anybody thinks. This is my night! I'm going to get delivered from this fear that's gripped me for so long.*

So I stood up for prayer, and Brother Hagin prayed for all of us to be delivered from fear. There were no instant manifestations. Nothing spectacular happened. I simply received the prayer by faith and believed in my heart that fear was not going to dog me anymore.

Of course, it always takes a test to prove whether we've really been set free from something. Not long after *Campmeeting*, I experienced that kind of test. My husband and I had to make a trip on a small, private aircraft. Not only that, but when we were ready to take off, the wind was blowing about 90 miles per hour!

My husband just gulped and looked to see my reaction. He must have thought, *Oh my goodness, what's my wife going to do in this tiny airplane with all of this wind?*

Meanwhile, I thought, *God, why did You allow me to be tested under such difficult circumstances?* But then I began to claim God's promises for my safety. I said, "Father, thank You that I'm going to be safe from the time I take off until the time I land. Thank You that You have not given me the spirit of fear, but of power and of love and of a sound mind (2 Tim. 1:7)."

Praise God, I flew in that small, private airplane and had no fear! I believe that was the ultimate test. It confirmed to me that I had been set free from the spirit of fear. And I've been free from the fear of flying ever since!

I want you to notice the first part of Second Timothy 1:7— "*God has not given us a spirit of fear* . . ." (NKJV). God is telling us in this scripture that fear is a spirit. If we allow it to, that spirit will get hold of us just as it got hold of me every time I had to fly. But the anointing of the Holy Spirit can set us free from the spirit of fear.

That verse also says that the spirit of fear does not come from God. If fear is a spirit and it does not come from God, then there is only one other source it could come from: the devil. And James 4:7 says, *"Resist the devil and he w.. _ from you"* (NKJV).

How do you resist the devil? One way you can resist the devil is by filling yourself up with God's Word in the area where Satan is attacking you. That's what I was doing when I meditated on and confessed God's Word concerning fear. And I was also using the Word as a powerful weapon—the Sword of the Spirit (Eph. 6:17)!

Put Your Armor On

The Sword of the Spirit is actually part of the whole armor of God, which is the armor the Lord has given us to help us stand against the attacks of Satan. I believe the reason why many Christians today are defeated in their walk with the Lord is, they don't keep their armor on. Let's read about this powerful spiritual armor in Ephesians chapter 6.

EPHESIANS 6:13–18 NKJV

13 Therefore take up the whole armor of God, that you may be able to withstand in the evil day, and having done all, to stand.

14 Stand therefore, having girded your waist with truth, having put on the breastplate of righteousness,

15 and having shod your feet with the preparation of the gospel of peace;

16 above all, taking the shield of faith with which you will be able to quench all the fiery darts of the wicked one.

17 And take the helmet of salvation, and the sword of the Spirit, which is the word of God;

18 praying always with all prayer and supplication in the Spirit. . . .

It's clear from these verses that God recognizes we're in a spiritual battle, and this battle is fiercer than any natural battle we will ever experience. The Lord also knows that our Enemy, the devil, is mean. Satan does not fight fair. But God has given us all the weapons we need to help us defeat the devil's attack.

Think about this for a moment. The United States Army wouldn't send a soldier into a war or some other type of conflict without issuing him any weapons, would they? How silly would that be?

Not only does a soldier need weapons, but he also needs ammunition. He needs to keep his weapons fully loaded, and he needs to have an extra supply of ammunition in case he has to reload his weapons during battle.

The same thing is true for us in the spiritual battle we're involved in here on this earth. We need to be armed with our spiritual weapons and have a full supply of ammunition. And the primary spiritual weapon God has given us is His Word.

If we're attacked by the devil and there's a supply of God's Word down on the inside of us, all we have to do is pull the trigger on our weapon, and out of our mouths will come the Sword of the Spirit—the Word of God.

I'm not talking about some kind of magic formula. The formula *is* the Word of God. We must keep our weapon loaded, and we must keep an extra supply of the ammunition of God's Word in our hearts. In other words, we must keep ourselves filled to overflowing with the Word of God.

I also want you to notice that Paul told us to put on the *whole* armor of God. That includes the belt of truth, the breastplate of righteousness, our gospel shoes, the shield of faith, the helmet of salvation, the sword of the Spirit, and, according to Ephesians 6:18, our prayers. It's so important for us to pray!

We can't put on just one or two parts of our armor and expect our weapons to work. We can't put on just the parts we like and leave off the others.

Some parts of the armor are a little heavier and more cumbersome than others. Some parts take more commitment to wear than other parts do. But what does the Word say? Put on the *whole* armor of God. Why? So we may be able to stand when we're attacked by fear or by the devil in some other area.

Are you wondering why you're having trouble standing in faith when you're attacked by Satan? Check your armor. Make certain that you've put on the whole armor of God, and keep your armor on.

It's so critical for us not to let down our guard. We must continually set a watch against the Enemy. Satan is not going to tell us when he's about to launch an attack. We are responsible to stay ready at all times, and that readiness includes putting on our armor.

People Scare Me

Another type of fear that I've had to overcome is the fear of speaking to a crowd of people. Just because I came from a minister's family and married a minister who is never at a loss for words doesn't mean I'm a natural-born orator.

To be perfectly honest, I'm not naturally eloquent. My husband can speak so beautifully at any given moment. Words just flow out of him. But I have not been endowed with that gift.

When I speak, I simply deliver my heart. Of course, I endeavor to do the best job of speaking that I possibly can. But the most important thing to me when I step behind the pulpit is being anointed with God's power. It's the anointing of the Holy Spirit that causes our words to touch people's hearts.

I never thought in a million years that I'd be speaking before large audiences as I am today. If anyone had told me I would do something like that, I would have said, "You're crazy. People scare me."

In fact, when God first began to deal with me about speaking publicly, I told Him, "But Lord, I love to minister to children. That's where I want to stay—in children's ministry!" Isn't it strange how God never seems to let us stay in our comfort zones? I believe that's because He wants us to rely on Him instead of on our own natural talents and abilities.

Do you know what the Lord said to me when I told Him I couldn't speak in front of large crowds of people? He told me, "Lynette, if I can use a donkey, surely I can use you." He was referring to the story in Numbers chapter 22 where God spoke to a man named Balaam through a donkey. And when the Lord said that to me, it straightened me right out.

So I learned Second Timothy 1:7 by heart and began to quote that verse every time I had to speak in front of a crowd—*"For God hath not given us the spirit of fear; but of power, and of love, and of a sound mind."* And over the years I've quoted that verse many times to help me deal with fear when I stand before an audience.

Sometimes I'm literally shaking in my boots when I step behind the pulpit. I often tell the Lord, "God, if You're expecting me to do anything without Your help, we're in a mess. All I know how to do is yield to You, and whatever You want to happen is what's going to happen."

I know the feeling of walking out onto the platform to minister and seeing the "men of the Sanhedrin" sitting on the front row. I'm talking about seeing a group of well-known senior ministers lined up right in front of me when I'm about to speak. When that has happened, my knees have gotten so weak and wobbly that I almost collapsed from fear.

One time I found out right before one of our crusades that a certain senior minister would attend the services. I became so upset when I heard the news that I actually made myself sick. The devil began to flash pictures through my mind of how this man was going to look when I stood in front of him to minister. And the fear was causing havoc in my mind.

When my husband heard me moaning and groaning that morning as I prepared to speak, he asked me, "Honey, what's wrong with you?"

"My stomach is killing me," I replied. There wasn't anything physically wrong with my stomach. I was just gripped with fear.

So my sweet husband said to me, "Well, let me pray for you." Thank God for a praying husband!

After he prayed, I quoted my favorite scripture, Philippians 4:13: "*I can do all things through Christ Who strengthens me*" (NKJV). And then I declared, "Devil, I'm going to give you a big black eye!"

Before the service was over that morning, I found myself laying hands on this particular minister and prophesying to him. If I had known that was going to happen, I would really have been fearful.

It turned out that this man was going through some difficulties, and he desperately needed a touch from the Lord. I didn't know anything about that, but the Lord knew. As I ministered to him, strength flowed into his body. I quoted Romans 8:11 to him: "If the Spirit of him that raised up Jesus from the dead dwells in you, he that raised up Christ from the dead will also quicken your mortal body. . . ."

When I began to minister along those lines, all the elders who had come to that meeting started jumping up and down and praising God because they were being renewed in the strength of the Lord. But that would not have taken place if I had failed to overcome the fear that was trying to get a grip on me.

If you're dealing with the fear of speaking, even if it's simply a fear of talking to your supervisor or someone else you need to talk to, I encourage you to rely on the Holy Spirit for help. The only way we can accomplish what we need to in life is through the power of the Holy Spirit. He gives us the power to speak. He gives us the strength. He is our Helper and our Standby. He will bring all things to our remembrance, whatever we need to say. (See John 14:26 Amplified.)

The scripture the Lord has used to encourage me in this area is Luke 12:12: *"For the Holy Ghost shall teach you in the same hour what ye ought to say."* If we learn to rely on the Holy Spirit, He will teach us what to say in all circumstances.

He'll teach us what to say when we need to talk to our banker. He'll teach us what to say when we have to talk to our supervisor on our job. He'll teach us what to say when we're negotiating a contract.

The Holy Spirit is the One Who can give you the boldness you need, and you will be astounded at some of the words that come out of your mouth. You may find yourself saying, "Where did that come from? I didn't even know that." No, you didn't. That's the Holy Spirit speaking through you. Wisdom and revelation will come forth through your mouth if you allow the Holy Spirit to inspire you when you speak.

Do You Want to Be Free?

When I talk about being set free from fear, I'm not talking about something I haven't experienced myself. All the stories I've shared with you in this chapter illustrate how the Lord has set me free. And there are still times when I have to deal with fear, because fear tries to come against all of us. Why? Satan specializes in fear.

When I first started trying to overcome my fears, I searched the Word for scriptures to help me resist fear. There are so many verses that can help us overcome any type of fear. Psalm 27:1 says, "*The Lord is my light and my salvation; whom shall I fear?*" And in John 14:27 Jesus said, "*Let not your heart be troubled, neither let it be afraid.*"

Hebrews 13:6 tells us, "*The Lord is my helper, and I will not fear what man shall do unto me.*" And Isaiah 41:10 says, "*Fear not, for I am with you; Be not dismayed, for I am your God . . .*" (NKJV).

I began to meditate on verses like these and say them out loud to build up my faith and drive out the fear. I used these scriptures as my weapon—the sword of the Spirit—and, as I said earlier, I claimed God's promises every time I had to fly on an airplane or do anything I was afraid to do. The more I meditated on and stood on God's Word, the less of a grip fear had on me.

I also knew what the Bible says in Isaiah 10:27—". . . *the yoke* [of bondage] *shall be destroyed because of the anointing."* Being tormented by fear can keep us in awful bondage. That's why I wanted to receive Brother Hagin's prayer to break that bondage.

If you're being tormented or bound by a spirit of fear, you know how horrible it can be. It may not be the fear of flying or the fear of speaking in front of a crowd, but any type of fear can keep you from accomplishing what God has planned for your life.

The Lord cares so much about you, and He wants you to be free. Are you ready to be set free from the spirit of fear? Then read through the following prayer, and pray it from your heart. As you pray, the anointing of the Holy Spirit will come upon you and break the yoke of fear and destroy the bondage of the devil. God will break that spirit of fear off your life.

In the Name of Jesus, I come against every power of darkness, every principality, and every spirit of fear. I declare that the power of every tormenting spirit is broken, in the Name of Jesus. The bondage is broken. There's a release in the spirit realm—a breakthrough of freedom!

The anointing of God's Spirit is setting me free! I let the peace of God rule in my heart, through the power of Jesus' Name. Amen.

I pray that you will "know that you know that you know" that God has given you a mighty victory. If the Enemy tries to put fear back on you, just remind him that Jesus Christ has set you free. John 8:36 says, *"If the Son [Jesus] sets you free, you will be free indeed"* (NIV). You will not be dominated by fear anymore!

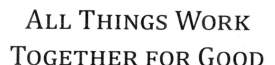

CHAPTER 11

ALL THINGS WORK
TOGETHER FOR GOOD

My favorite Bible story is the life of Joseph. When I start reading it, I can't stop until I've finished the whole story—and it's 14 chapters long (Genesis 37–50). I love Joseph's story because it's such an inspiration to me. It proves that no matter what happens in our lives, God can turn things around for our good.

You see, Joseph was one of the greatest dreamers who ever lived. But every time he had a dream, somebody came along and tried to burst his bubble. For many years, all Joseph experienced was one devastating setback after another. Yet he put his trust in the Lord, and God turned even the worst situations around for Joseph's good.

As Joseph was growing up, he was his father Jacob's favorite son. One day his father had a special gift made for him—a wonderful coat of many colors (Gen. 37:3–4). When his brothers saw that coat, they had a fit! They were so jealous of Joseph that they couldn't say a kind word to him.

Then Joseph began to have some very strange dreams. First, he dreamed that he and his brothers were out in the field, tying up bundles of wheat. Joseph's bundle stood up above all the others, and his brothers' bundles bowed to him.

You can imagine how that dream "thrilled" his brothers when he told them about it. The Bible says they hated him more than ever. Actually, it would have been wiser for Joseph to keep the dream to himself. But he didn't.

Later Joseph had another dream, and in this dream, the sun, moon, and eleven stars (representing his father, mother, and eleven brothers) bowed down to him. When Joseph told his father about the dream, at first Jacob scolded him, saying, *"Will your mother and I and your brothers actually come and bow to the ground before you?"* (Gen. 37:10 NLT). But Jacob wondered in his heart what the dreams really meant.

One day Joseph's brothers had gone out into the fields to tend their father's flocks, and Jacob sent Joseph to check on them. When they saw him coming, they cried out, "Here comes the dreamer!" and they immediately began plotting to kill him.

The oldest brother, Reuben, pleaded with them not to kill the boy. Instead he told them to throw Joseph into an empty cistern out in the wilderness. The Bible says that he was secretly planning to rescue his brother.

As soon as Joseph got close enough for them to get their hands on him, they took his beautiful coat from him and threw him into the cistern. A short time later, they spotted a caravan of Ishmaelite traders passing nearby, so they decided to sell Joseph into slavery. Then they smeared goat's blood on his coat and told his father that wild animals had devoured him.

By this time, I'm sure Joseph must have wondered how on earth his dreams could ever become a reality. But he discovered something powerful through those experiences—something that will help all of us as we pursue the dreams God has placed in our hearts. He discovered that the key word in following God's plan is *trust*!

Joseph Had Many Opportunities to Let Go of His Dreams

When the Ishmaelites arrived in Egypt, they sold Joseph to Potiphar, the captain of the palace guard. He was a very powerful man and extremely close to Pharaoh.

Genesis 39:2 says, *"The Lord was with Joseph, so he succeeded in everything he did as he served in the home of his Egyptian master"* (NLT). Potiphar was highly pleased with Joseph and put him in charge of his whole household. Even in the midst of captivity, Joseph had favor and was wonderfully blessed by the Lord. Not only that, but God began to bless Potiphar's entire household for Joseph's sake. Even his crops and livestock prospered.

The Bible also tells us that Joseph was a handsome young man. It wasn't long until Potiphar's wife tried to seduce Joseph. He refused to bow to her demands, but she just kept on pressuring him.

One day when none of the other servants were around, she grabbed Joseph by his cloak and propositioned him again. He managed to get away from her, but when he ran out of the room, she was still clutching his garment in her hands.

She screamed for her servants, and when they rushed to see what had happened, she accused Joseph of trying to rape her. Later, she showed Joseph's coat to Potiphar and told him her concocted story. He was so furious that he had Joseph thrown into prison.

Once again, Joseph must have wondered how his dreams could ever come to pass. He was probably shocked that things could have turned out so badly when he was just trying to live for the Lord and do what was right.

Joseph could have had a great, big pity party as he sat there in Pharaoh's prison. He could have said, "God, why did You allow this to happen to me?" But he kept his heart pure and his attitude right, and he made the best of the situation.

Do you know what happened because of Joseph's positive attitude and his faith and trust in the Lord? God turned things around for his good! And you and I have a powerful promise in Romans 8:28 that says God will do the same thing for us: *"And we know that all things work together for good to them that love God, to them who are the called according to his purpose."* We can believe, just as Joseph did, that God will bring His best out of every situation.

'Interpreting Dreams Is God's Business'

Joseph found favor wherever he was, even in the middle of Pharaoh's prison. The Bible says that the Lord made him the favorite of the warden, and he was put in charge of all the other prisoners. Actually, the warden made him second in command over the affairs of the whole prison.

One day Pharaoh flew into a rage and threw his baker and butler into prison. During the night, each one of them had a dream, and the next morning Joseph noticed how worried and upset they were. When he asked them what was wrong, they told him about their dreams. *"Interpreting dreams is God's business,"* he replied. *"Go ahead and tell me your dreams"* (Gen. 40:8 NLT).

So Joseph interpreted the butler's dream first, and his dream had a good interpretation—a "happy ending." It revealed that he would be released from prison in only three days and restored to his former position with Pharaoh.

The baker got so excited when he heard the interpretation of the butler's dream that he decided to share his dream with Joseph too. But his dream did not have a happy ending. In fact, Joseph told him that in three days Pharaoh was going to have him executed.

Sure enough, three days later, both men were released from prison and brought before Pharaoh. Pharaoh restored the butler to his former position, but the baker was executed, just as Joseph had said he would be. Joseph had asked the butler to put in a good word for him with Pharaoh, but the butler was so thrilled about getting out of prison that he promptly forgot about Joseph.

Joseph could have gotten mad. He could have become frustrated and said, "God doesn't love me anymore." But he just kept on being faithful to the Lord. He refused to allow bitterness to creep in. And God continued to turn things around for Joseph's good.

It was two more years before Pharaoh had a dream that none of his wise men or magicians could interpret. All of a sudden the butler remembered the young Hebrew in prison who had a gift from God of interpreting dreams.

Joseph was summoned by Pharaoh, and I want you to notice his humility when Pharaoh began to talk to him about interpreting his dream. Pharaoh said, *"'I have heard it said of you that when you hear a dream you can interpret it'"* (Gen. 41:15 NIV).

Joseph replied, *"'I cannot do it, . . . but God will give Pharaoh the answer he desires'"* (v. 16). When Joseph interpreted Pharaoh's dream, he told him there would be seven years of plenty in Egypt followed by seven years of devastating famine. Then he advised Pharaoh to appoint a wise governor over the land to gather up the crops during the years of plenty and put them in storehouses for the years of famine.

Pharaoh was so impressed by Joseph's wisdom that he appointed the young Hebrew to that position, making him second-in-command in Egypt, subordinate only to Pharaoh. At last, it seemed that Joseph's dreams were going to become a reality.

Joseph was 17 years old when he was sold into slavery, and he was 30 years old when he was brought before Pharaoh to interpret his dream. For 13 long years he had carried his God-given dreams in his heart, unfulfilled. And it was still several more years before his dreams came to pass.

I believe the account of Joseph is the original "turn it around" story in the Bible. He experienced many setbacks and attacks of the devil, but because Joseph kept his attitude right and stayed close to the Lord, God continually turned things around for his good.

When famine struck the land of Canaan, Joseph's brothers came to Egypt seeking food. They didn't recognize him at first, but they bowed down to him, just as his dreams had revealed that they would.

Finally, Joseph told his brothers who he was, and they were terrified of him at first. But instead of punishing them for selling him into slavery, he forgave them.

I want you to read what Joseph said to his brothers in Genesis 50:20, ". . . *you meant evil against me; BUT GOD MEANT IT FOR GOOD, in order to . . . save many people alive*" (NKJV). Joseph realized that God had sent him to Egypt ahead of his brothers to save their whole family. At last, all of his dreams became a reality!

I want you to think about some of the things that may have befallen you in the past. Someone may have done something that hurt you terribly. They may have even meant to harm you. But God is saying to you that He will turn it around for your good.

We may not understand why things happen a certain way in our lives, but we can always declare by faith, "Everything is working together for my good, because that's what God said in Romans 8:28!"

Suddenly My Dream Seemed to Vanish

Like Joseph, I felt a calling from the Lord early in my life—a calling to be in the ministry. Because I had grown up in a pastor's home, I had always been involved in the ministry.

My dad was an extremely nurturing pastor. He loved his people and he was always there for his congregation. It was through his example that I developed that same kind of love for people. I truly love to minister to people, listen to their problems, and help them with the wisdom God gives me.

From an early age, I realized that if I was going to spend very much time with my dad, I would have to hook up with his vision. So from about 9 years old, I became an active volunteer in the church.

I was right there to help my dad write the bulletin or transcribe his sermons, and I also learned to play the organ.

I wanted to do whatever I could to be part of his life, and in doing that I learned to love the ministry. It became second nature to me.

After Ken and I were married, I played the piano and worked the book table when we were traveling in the ministry. If we had pastoral duties, I worked in every area of the church—the choir, children's church, or wherever else I was needed.

But then the day came for me, just as it did for Joseph, when it seemed as if my dream of being in the ministry had suddenly vanished. For about two years, there was no place for me in the ministry.

I had two small children at home, and they were at the age when they needed a lot of my attention. That meant my entire role in life was strictly to minister to my husband and children.

Of course, I had always tried not to neglect those areas. But I had been so busy and active in the ministry that I had never been able to relate to the frustrations of a stay-at-home mom. All of a sudden, I could relate to those feelings all too well.

I really wanted to take care of my husband and family, but that wasn't *all* I wanted to do. Like Joseph's, my life certainly wasn't how I had pictured it. I knew I had a calling from the Lord to be in the ministry, yet there was no ministry for me anywhere in sight.

As I stayed at home day after day cleaning my house, straightening my closets, organizing my kitchen, and buying all of my groceries for the month, I would suddenly find myself sitting there, saying, "What do I do now?" All the time, I was thinking, *Dear Lord, what good could possibly come out of this?*

Now, for someone else that might have been a completely wonderful and fulfilling time, but those were dark years for me. Really, that period in my life seemed to be a season of "captivity."

So I did what I've always done during a rough time—I prayed. I talked to my Heavenly Father—and God turned those dark times around for my good.

During that period, my prayer life developed to the point where I told the Lord, "If my entire ministry for the rest of my life is to pray, I'm totally committed to that." I remember having so many precious times with the Lord during those years, praying for my children and my husband, and praying for God to show us His plan for our lives. And many of the things we've done in the ministry in recent years were birthed during that time of intense prayer.

As I prayed, the Lord said to me, "Lynette, I'm teaching you some things and taking you down some paths so you will have compassion for those who are experiencing the same things that you've experienced." That was also when he began to speak to me about ministering to women, which I'll share more about in the next chapter.

One reason I was able to come victoriously through those experiences was, I had been hearing the Word of God preached two times a day as I traveled with my husband and father-in-law in the crusades. As a result, my spirit was strong in the Word. Even though the devil was attacking my mind, I knew what I needed to do—get into God's Word and pray and commune with my Heavenly Father. And that's exactly what I did.

During those wonderful times with the Lord, He taught me so many things about prayer. And He told me that in my later ministry, one thing I would do was to lead people into His presence through prayer.

Just as He promised, God has anointed me in recent years to minister to many people on the subject of prayer. I've been able to help them enjoy the presence of the Lord and receive God's answers when they pray.

God turned around what seemed to be a dark, depressing experience and caused it to work for my good. He also caused it to work for the good of my family and of all the people He's allowed me to minister to over the years. If we'll put our trust in the Lord and be sensitive to His Spirit, He can turn everything that happens to us around for our good.

Is This a Promotion or a Demotion?

My husband's work as an associate pastor in west Texas was one of our first adventures in the ministry. Things went so well for us during that time. We were just beginning to prosper, and everything seemed to be working for our good.

Then, all of a sudden, the Lord said, "It's time for a change." We went from being associate pastors in west Texas to being associate pastors for my dad.

When we looked at that situation in the natural, it did not appear that things were working for our good. We took a 50 percent pay cut to go to work for my dad!

All at once, we were making half of what we had been making out in west Texas. I don't know about you, but when my salary is cut in half, it can drastically affect my budget—especially when my bills had previously been figured on twice the amount of income.

But we knew we were following the Lord and doing His will, and He faithfully continued to bless us. During that time, I helped my husband and dad in the ministry, but I also went to cosmetology school and worked as a hairdresser.

The Lord just supernaturally blessed my little business. Even though I worked only part time, I made as much as the other hairdressers around me who worked full time. The Lord was truly blessing and prospering our lives.

So we began to relax and say, "Thank You, God, for your blessings. We appreciate so much what You've done for us."

Then, all of a sudden, the Lord tapped us on the shoulder again and said, "It's time to take another step." But this step seemed even worse than the last one. Not only was our salary cut in half *again*, but the position my husband took didn't include *any* preaching responsibilities.

I'm talking about when he first became crusade director for his dad at Kenneth Hagin Ministries. He was involved in all the behind-the-scenes responsibilities, but he didn't even darken the pulpit, other than to make announcements. It looked like a real demotion for him. Meanwhile, we were thinking, *God, every time we take a step to follow Your plan, our salary is cut in half!*

What we were doing didn't make any sense at all in the natural. But we knew it was what God had called us to do. And we also believed what the Bible says in Psalm 37:23: *"The steps of a good man* [or woman] *are ordered by the Lord, And He delights in his way"* (NKJV). We were trusting God that He was ordering our steps.

Sometimes it looked as if we were in captivity, just as Joseph was. It certainly looked as if God was taking us on the "long cut" instead of the shortcut to our destiny. But, like Joseph, we were being prepared by the Lord for a future that was far greater than anything we could possibly have imagined.

Ultimately, the dreams God had placed in our hearts were fulfilled. But the steps we took to get there were not the ones we anticipated. And that's what gets us into trouble so many times in life. We try to interpret God's plan instead of walking it out, and then we get it all in a mess.

Thank God, it's not our job to interpret His plan. It's our job to let Him *unfold* the plan. Then we can walk out His divine plan—step by step.

Keep Your Eyes on Your Heavenly Father

If you want to fulfill God's plan, you have to focus on the Lord and not on the setbacks and obstacles that come across your path. Joseph could have focused on and magnified all the bad things happening in his life. But he didn't. Ken and I could have gotten hung up on having to take a pay cut every time we took another step to serve God. But we didn't.

Like Joseph, we kept our eyes on the Lord, even when we had no idea why He was taking us along a certain path. And He turned every situation around for our good.

No matter how difficult our circumstances, we must not focus on the bad or incomprehensible things that are happening. God is saying to us, "Keep your eyes on your Deliverer! He will turn things around for you."

Remember, our Heavenly Father is faithful. We can trust Him to do what He said He would do, whether it's showing us the next step in following His plan or healing us of an incurable disease. Our Father is in the business of performing His Word!

CHAPTER 12

THE WAITING ZONE

Have you ever been tempted to try to rush through life—to hurry up so you could get to the "good parts"? I have. But to follow God's plan and fulfill our divine destiny, we have to go through different seasons.

Psalm 1:3 (NIV) tells us that the godly person is *"like a tree planted by streams of water, which yields its fruit in season. . . ."* The key words in that verse are *in season.* We get so thrilled when we think about the prospect of yielding fruit. But it's easy to get discouraged as we wait for our season of fruitfulness.

I've never planted a garden, but my dad used to plant one every year. However, just because he planted some seed in the ground didn't mean that he was going to reap a harvest the next day, or even the next week or month. The fruit came in the right season. And if you tried to harvest the fruit at the wrong season, you might get a stomachache from eating unripe fruit!

Just as we go through various natural seasons, we also go through different seasons spiritually. With the spiritual seasons of life, I like some better than others. And the "waiting season" is one that I don't particularly care for.

Really, waiting is something that most of us don't like to do. We've been trained in today's society to expect everything to happen instantly. We don't want to wait for our dinner at a restaurant. We either pull into the drive-through and order a fast-food meal or we cook something in the microwave oven. We want everything in a hurry! But God is never in a hurry.

Why does God make us wait at times? I believe in some cases it's because He's "seasoning" us. What do I mean by that? Well, if you've ever cooked a pot of beans, you know how much better they taste if you let them simmer for a while. When you cook those beans slowly, they absorb the seasonings much better.

When we find ourselves in the "waiting zone," it may be because God is seasoning us. He may be preparing us for the things He's called us to do. And it's extremely important for us to learn how to wait.

Isaiah 40:31 says, *"They that wait upon the Lord shall renew their strength; they shall mount up with wings as eagles; they shall run, and not be weary; and they shall walk, and not faint."* If you're suffering from weariness and you don't have a lot of strength, you can be renewed and refreshed as you wait on the Lord. But I know from my own experience that sometimes it's hard to wait.

Twenty-Five Years of Waiting

As I mentioned in the last chapter, the Lord told me many years ago that He wanted me to minister to women. And I thought, *Minister to women! God, that's the* last *thing I want to do*!

To be perfectly honest, I detested women's meetings. First of all, every women's meeting I had ever gone to always seemed to turn into a pity party, and I don't like pity parties. I like victory parties. Also, many of the women's meetings I knew anything about had a bad reputation—a reputation of being flaky.

I was so thankful that the women's meetings in our church were held on Tuesday mornings—a time when I had to be at work. That gave me a wonderful excuse not to attend.

So when the Lord began to deal with me about ministering to women, I said, "But Lord, I don't like women's meetings. They're not my cup of tea. And besides, I don't want to be known as a flaky woman."

For several years, I wrestled with the Lord over His calling to minister to women. Every time I prayed about it, I would agonize and say, "Lord, please! I don't want to do that!"

Then God said something very powerful to me. He told me, "There are mighty things that I need these women to accomplish for Me, but they can't do it if they're having pity parties and feeling sorry for themselves. I want you to pick them up and put them on the road of victory instead of the road of despair."

Finally I surrendered to God's call to minister to women, and as soon as I did, the Lord told me to wait. Oh my! But there's usually a waiting time concerning the things God speaks to our hearts. There's a right time and a wrong time to move on those things. If we try to accomplish them in the wrong season, they won't succeed.

I was 31 years old when God first spoke to me about ministering to women, and I thought, *When I reach 40, that's when I'll begin to fulfill that call.* But 40 came and went and the Lord didn't say, "Go ye and minister to women." That was just fine with me, so I thought, *Maybe You forgot about what You said to me, God.*

Then my 50th birthday came and went, and I still didn't hear a "Go ye." *Whoo, God, that's wonderful!* I thought. *Maybe You really* did *change Your mind about calling me to minister to women.*

It wasn't until I was 55 years old that the Lord finally said to me, "Now is the time to minister to women." That was in early 2001, and I told Him, "God, if You want me to do this, I'm asking You to give me the plan."

The first thing the Lord said to me was, "I will gather around you an army of women." All of a sudden, I began to feel an excitement in my spirit. Since my husband had served in the U.S. Army and loves the Army, the Army is close to my heart. I immediately told the Lord, "Yes, I can lead an army of women if that's what You want me to do."

Then He continued, "These women shall be women of balance, longing to know how to balance womanhood, motherhood, and the assignment which I've called them to do. You shall lead the way . . . for these women have come, even as Esther came, for such a time as this."

When I heard those words, something exploded on the inside of me. I thought, *Yes, Lord, many of us have already accomplished something for You, but You've still kept us on the back burner to do something great for You in this hour!*

Then the Lord began to lay out before me the details of the first women's conference, and He even told me who He wanted to speak. When I tried to contact one of the ladies He mentioned, she was on a ship out in the ocean. You're not supposed to be able to connect with someone by cell phone when they're on a ship, but nothing is too hard for my God. We did connect, and she accepted my invitation to be a speaker at my first conference.

Another one of the ladies God mentioned to me as a speaker was in Italy at the time. But that didn't matter to the Lord either. He hand-picked those ladies, and all of them were available to speak at the first *Kindle the Flame® Women's Conference.*

Then God told me, "This is the date you are to hold the conference," and it was toward the end of September. So our first conference was held right after the 9/11 terrorist attack on America. Little did I know what condition our nation would be in at that particular moment. But God knew. He's never caught by surprise.

At that time, much of the transportation system across America was shut down. Planes were grounded. Security was heightened. And people were calling us from all over the country, asking, "Are you cancelling the meeting?"

Does God ever cancel His plans? No! We weren't about to cancel that conference and let the Enemy win a victory. I told my staff, "God will make a way for these ladies to come."

That first year approximately 1,400 ladies attended the conference, including 100 ladies from the New York City area. We were told it would be impossible to get to Tulsa from New York, but they found a way!

I stood on the platform that first night with tears in my eyes, because I saw before me an army of women, just as God had spoken to me about so many years before. It had been 25 years since He first told me that I would minister to women. But even though all of those years had passed, He still fulfilled every word He had spoken to my heart.

If I had decided to have a women's conference in the wrong season, at the wrong time, the plan of God would not have been carried out. But because I waited on God's timing, the women's conference was a great success. It's so important for us not to rush through the "waiting seasons" of life. It's absolutely vital for us to learn to wait on the Lord.

Give Me My Mountain

I remember the story of Caleb, who waited 45 years for God's promise to become a reality. In Numbers chapter 13, Moses sent Joshua, Caleb, and 10 other spies to explore the Promised Land. The 10 brought back a bad report. They said, "It's a good land, but there are giants there. And we are like grasshoppers in their sight."

Only Joshua and Caleb brought back a good report. They said, "With the Lord's help, we can take the land!" But the children of Israel were so focused on the giants that they couldn't see the delivering power of God. So they wound up wandering around in the wilderness for another 40 years.

After Moses died, Joshua was chosen to lead the people into the Promised Land. Now Caleb could have gotten jealous about that. The report he had brought back was just as good as Joshua's, wasn't it? He could have wondered why he didn't get to lead the people. If this situation had occurred today, some people would have been jealous because God was using someone else other than them, and they would have lost their blessing.

But Caleb didn't get mad. He didn't get jealous. He just kept following the Lord with all of his heart. He kept his eye on what God had promised him, and he kept walking on the path God had planned for his life. And that's what the Lord wants all of us to do.

At the end of those 45 years of waiting, Caleb came to Joshua to claim his inheritance—his mountain.

JOSHUA 14:7,10–12 NIV

7 I was forty years old when Moses . . . sent me from Kadesh Barnea to explore the land. . . .

10 . . . [The Lord] has kept me alive for forty-five years . . . while Israel moved about in the desert. So here I am today, eighty-five years old!

11 I am still as strong today as the day Moses sent me out; . . .

12 Now give me this hill country that the Lord promised me that day. You yourself heard then that the Anakites [giants] were there and their cities were large and fortified, but, the Lord helping me, I will drive them out just as he said."

Praise God, Caleb recognized the facts about the dangers that awaited him in the hill country, but he was armed with the greater facts—the facts of God's Word. He was armed with God's promise that He would help Caleb, and Caleb took his mountain.

The Lord will help you receive what He's promised you too! It doesn't matter what your age is, or how long you've waited for God's promise. You're armed with the greater facts of God's Word, and Psalm 37:5 says, *"Commit your way to the Lord, Trust also in Him, And He shall bring it to pass"* (NKJV).

I Thought I Misheard God

I've had many experiences of waiting for God's promises to me to be fulfilled. Besides waiting 25 years to begin ministering to women, I also waited 20 years for my God-given dream of being a pastor's wife to become a reality.

Even as a young child, I knew that I was called to be a pastor's wife. When Ken and I were married in December of 1965, I thought, *Okay, Lord, the things You have called me to and prepared me for will now come to pass.* But they didn't.

Five years passed, and my dream of becoming a pastor's wife still hadn't become a reality. Another five years went by, and then 10 years, and the dream still had not materialized. So I thought, *Maybe I misheard God.*

Finally, I told the Lord, "The desire to be a pastor's wife is burning in my heart, but it doesn't seem to be happening. Would you please take the pastor's heart out of me."

It took several years for me to pray the pastor's heart out of my spirit, because it was so strong in me. But I finally lost that desire. Then, for the next few years I was completely happy working with my husband in the ministry. I really loved it. I remember thinking, *I was crazy to want to be a pastor's wife.*

About 20 years after Ken and I were married, all of a sudden, the Word of the Lord came to us through a powerful man of faith, Lester Sumrall. It was in March of 1985 when Brother Sumrall prophesied to my husband, saying, "I see something like a light that is covering the entire campus of RHEMA, and the dynamics and the movement and the direction of that great thrust of God will come out of *this man* [my husband] . . . and God is making and creating and forming a powerful spiritual leader. . . ." Little did we know that that prophecy involved starting our own church!

At the time, a prayer group on the RHEMA campus felt God stirring them to pray for my husband to have a pastor's heart. Well, that didn't seem to fit into the plan at all. But thank God for faithful "pray-ers" who are sensitive to the Holy Spirit. They just kept on praying, and they didn't tell a soul what they were praying about.

In June of that year we traveled to South Africa for a meeting. The evangelist's anointing which usually operated through my husband wasn't manifesting during those services. Why? Because the Lord was birthing a pastor's heart in him.

Finally, after about a month or so, Ken said to me, "Honey, I don't know what you're going to think about this, but the Lord is dealing with me about starting a church."

At first, I was thrilled that I really had heard from God about our calling to be pastors. I had just gotten off on the timing. But then I thought, *Oh my goodness! I have prayed the pastor's heart out of my heart, and now I have to pray it back in!* But when you're dealing with something that's been close to your heart, it doesn't take long for God to put that back into your spirit.

In October of 1985 we held our first service at RHEMA Bible Church. I had thought we would pastor a church of about 300 members, but God thought something different.

He gave us a church of 8,000 members! His dreams are so much bigger than our dreams, and His timing is certainly different from ours. I had waited 20 years for that dream to become a reality, and it finally did. It's not too late for *your* dream to come to pass either.

It may be 20 or 30 years or more since God spoke something to your heart. Perhaps you dream has been on the back burner for so long that you think you've missed it. You may be like I was. Perhaps you didn't have the timing quite right. Even though I didn't have the timing right, the calling was still the same. And it's never too late for God to fulfill the things He's spoken to our hearts.

We're All Geared Up, and God Says to Wait

The plan of God for our lives doesn't come to pass overnight. There's always a waiting process. We usually want to jump from step one to step 50, but there's a waiting and a proving time. There's a molding time. And none of us likes that.

We're a lot like the disciples were when Jesus told them to wait in Jerusalem for the promise of the Holy Spirit (Acts 1:4–5). They immediately began to ask Him questions about the date and time the kingdom was going to be restored by the Father. But Jesus told them, "*It is not for you to know the times or dates the Father has set by his own authority*" (v. 7 NIV).

Isn't that just like us? We get so involved in trying to interpret prophecies and figure out exactly when the Lord is coming back that we neglect the ministry God has called us to. He wants each of us to take our place in His kingdom—the place where He wants us to be *right now.*

In some cases, we may find ourselves spending more time in the waiting zone than we ever imagined. When that happens, we need to be even more sensitive to the Lord and let Him direct our *every* step. It's so important not to miss God's timing. The right plan at the wrong time is still not the will of God.

Sometimes we get tired and frustrated when we've been sitting on the back burner of life for a long time. Our calling seems to be dim and we feel as if all of those years have been wasted.

Those years in the waiting zone have not been wasted. God has led you through many experiences to bring you to this moment. Don't throw those experiences to the wind or try to forget them. They're part of your training and calling. They're part of what has made you the person God created you to be. And you'll be amazed at how those experiences will help you minister to the people God brings across your path.

When you find yourself in the waiting zone, spend time communing with your Heavenly Father and focus on hearing His voice. Let it be a time of refreshing and renewing of your strength. Then you'll be ready to rise as on eagle's wings when the Lord says to you, "My child, let's go! Now the time has come!"

CHAPTER 13

≈

I'M AN ETERNAL SONGBOOK

Several years ago my husband and I invited our pastoral staff over to our house and we wound up playing a game that involves drawing pictures. As soon as somebody suggested playing that game, my mind went back to the experiences I had in art class during my school days. There were times when I would burst into tears because I simply could not draw.

One of our associate pastors who was a pretty good artist said, "Oh, everybody can draw."

But I told him, "I know my strengths and my weaknesses. Art is not my strength. In fact, it's one of my biggest weaknesses."

When my turn came, I drew my picture and it was pretty bad. Our associate pastor looked at me and gasped, "That's horrible!" You talk about having a poor self-image. After he said that, I *really* had one. But the truth is, art is just not my talent.

Another time when the pastoral staff was at our house, we decided to play a musical game. You were supposed to select a word and then sing a song with that word in it.

When we played *that* game, I always thought of exactly the right song. That's because I knew so many Christian songs from being involved in church all of my life. Later, one of the pastors nicknamed me "The Eternal Songbook," because knowing all of those songs *is* one of my talents.

To fulfill God's plan for our lives, we have to learn to be content with being who He created us to be and having the talents He's given us. Instead of criticizing ourselves and demeaning God's creation, we should say to the Lord as David did, "... *Marvelous are Your works* ..." (Psalm 139:14 NKJV). We should tell Him, "God, You did a good job."

I'm reminded of the parable Jesus told in Matthew 25:14–30 of three servants who were each given a certain number of talents. In that particular story, a talent was a form of money, but the story also illustrates the importance of using the natural talents God has given us.

In that parable, one of the servants was given five talents, and he invested them and brought back 10 talents to his master. One was given two talents, which he also invested, and he brought his master back four talents.

But the servant who was given only one talent dug a hole in the ground and buried it. He hid his talent and didn't use it for his lord. And his master was furious with him.

So many times we're like the servant who was given one talent. We don't do anything with the talent God has given us because we're constantly dwelling on the talents we don't have, or we're focusing on our insufficiencies or what we can't do. In some cases we're not using our talents because we're jealous of the talents the Lord has given someone else. God wants us to be thankful for the talents He's given us as well as appreciate those He's given other people.

Let me give you another example of what I'm talking about here. My husband sometimes thinks I'm weird because one thing I like to do is organize everything. And I also like to write procedures. He thinks that's weird because doing those things is work to him. He is not an organizer by nature, and he doesn't like procedures.

On the other hand, my husband doesn't mind making decisions, and after he makes them, he doesn't worry about whether people like him. But making decisions and handling conflict stresses me out, because I want everybody to like me.

Each one of us has our own special gifts and talents, and we need to appreciate the gifts God has given to us as well as the gifts He's given to others. We wouldn't be happy being clones.

God made you just the way He wanted you to be. If you're short, be content with that. If you're tall, be content with being tall. It's important for us not to criticize God's workmanship. He made you perfect according to His specifications. He made you exactly the way you need to be to fulfill His plan.

Now, we still should try to improve ourselves. But the Enemy would love for us to focus on our "I can'ts" instead of our "I cans." No. We need to focus on our being ". . . *fearfully and wonderfully made...*" (Ps. 139:14). And we need to remember that God is the Master of taking ordinary people and doing extraordinary things with their lives. Besides, it's not about our great characteristics or abilities. It's about our great God!

Content in a Tiny Garage Apartment

We need to be content not only with who God created us to be but also with our present situation in life. The Apostle Paul made a powerful statement in Philippians 4:11–13—"*... I have learned to be content whatever the circumstances. I know what it is to be in need, and I know what it is to have plenty. I have learned the secret of being content in any and every situation, whether well fed or hungry, whether living in plenty or in want. I can do everything through him who gives me strength*" (NIV).

In our day, so many Christians are not content in their present situation. If they're single, they want to be married. Or if they're married, sometimes they think they want to be single. Or they're dissatisfied with their job, until suddenly that job is eliminated in a layoff. Then they really appreciate the job they just lost!

One of the first apartments my husband and I lived in right after we were married wasn't exactly ideal. We had taken an associate pastor's job in a small town out in west Texas. There was very limited housing in the town, and most of the apartments and houses that were available wouldn't allow pets.

Now, we didn't have any children at the time, but we had a little poodle named Pierre. Pierre was my only "child" before our children were born, and that little dog was precious to me. So I started calling all over town, asking people with rental property, "Do you allow pets?"

Over and over the answer came, "No, we don't."

By then I was getting desperate. I told the Lord, "God, You said You would grant the desires of our hearts (Ps. 37:4). You called us to come to this town, and I know that You can provide the housing we need so we can keep our little dog. Please show us what to do and give us favor."

All of a sudden, I ran across an ad for a garage apartment for rent. I had no idea what the apartment looked like, but I called the people and asked them, "Do you permit pets?"

"We never have," they replied. But I just kept on talking.

"Well, we have a little poodle," I told them. "Would you consider letting us have our poodle in your garage apartment?"

"Why don't you come over and meet us?" they replied.

They were an elderly couple, and the apartment they had for rent was literally a garage that had been converted into an apartment. It had a living room, kitchen, bathroom, and bedroom, all in the tiny space of about 20 feet by 20 feet. But I didn't care where I lived as long as my husband and my poodle were with me.

So we took our poodle and went to talk to this couple. They immediately fell in love with our little dog. "We've never done this before," they told us, "and we don't know why we're doing it now. But we're going to let you rent our apartment."

That tiny garage apartment was not the ideal place for us to live, but I was so happy there. I remember many times when we would let our little dog go outside for a few minutes, and then he would suddenly turn up missing. Later we found out that this couple was letting him into their house. When we went away for the weekend, they loved to keep our dog for us. And for many years after we moved away, this precious couple sent a Christmas card to our little poodle, Pierre Hagin!

It wasn't my ultimate goal to live for the next 50 years in that tiny garage apartment, but I didn't grumble about it. I was just thankful for a place to live that would allow me to have my dog. And when we're following God's plan for our lives, it's important for us to be content in the situations we find ourselves in along His path.

Content in a 31-Foot-Long Motor Home

I remember another situation where the Lord gave me the grace to be content in spite of some very challenging circumstances. When Ken and I traveled in the ministry, we lived in a 31-foot-long motor home.

All of my life I have been a homebody. I love to be at home. As I was growing up, my family didn't travel much, and I couldn't stand to travel.

When Ken and I began traveling with his dad in the crusades, not only were we doing something that I didn't particularly like to do, but we were also gone from home for several months at a time. And while we were on the road, we lived in that motor home with our 3-year-old son.

That was a golden opportunity for me to learn how to be content, no matter the circumstances. And I certainly found out how committed I was to the Lord.

Even after our daughter was born, we continued to travel from crusade to crusade in that motor home with two small children. But we were happy and contented. As a matter of fact, those were some of the happiest days for our kids. They absolutely loved that motor home!

We would hurry to get to the next meeting a few days early, just so we would have a couple of days to see the sights with the kids. They loved those days on the road, and they both still love to travel. They still get excited when they talk about those good times.

I believe that following God's plan for our lives won't cause our families to be neglected. Instead, it will cause them to be blessed. And if four people are crowded into a 31-foot-long motor home for months at a time, we can still do what Paul said in Philippians 4:11—we can be content, no matter what.

You Can Escape From the Questioning Realm

One of the biggest obstacles to our contentment is constantly questioning the Lord. Of course, God doesn't mind if we ask Him for specific answers when we're troubled about something. But He doesn't want us trapped in the questioning realm. Thank God, He has an escape route for us—and it's called *trust.*

One of my favorite scriptures in the whole Bible is Proverbs 3:5–6. It says, *"Trust in the Lord with all your heart, And lean not on your own understanding; In all your ways acknowledge Him, And He shall direct your paths"* (NKJV). When I was a teenager, a minister of the Gospel gave me a Bible and he wrote these verses in it. As a result, this passage has been important to me for many years.

So many times, I've had to choose not to get into the arena of questioning the Lord. Oh, I wanted to question Him. I wanted to say, "Why, God, why?" But I chose to put my trust in Him, regardless of the path I was traveling. I had to put my confidence in the Word of God and believe that He would perform the things He had promised me.

Have you come to the place where you're trusting the Lord with all of your heart? Are you acknowledging Him in all of your ways and refusing to lean to your own understanding?

Setbacks and adverse circumstances come to all of us at one time or another. But the people who have the hardest time overcoming the circumstances of life are the ones who continually question the Lord. They're saying, "Why, God, why? Why did this happen to me? I've stood on Your Word. I've prayed. I've lived a godly life. Why am I going through this?"

Proverbs 3:5–6 tells us not to try to figure out those things. Instead, we are to put our trust in the Lord and know that He will bring us through the trials and rough places of life.

You may be wondering why you're going through some of the things you're dealing with right now. But the Lord is saying to you, "Trust Me."

You may not understand why you're living in that town at this particular time. But the Lord still says to you, "Trust Me."

You may have so many "whys" that you've almost lost your confidence in the Lord. But God is saying to you this very moment, "Trust Me."

Remember, you can't do anything about what has already happened, so just fix your eyes on the goal and press on toward God's calling. He wants us to press toward the future as the Apostle Paul urges us to do in Philippians 3:13–14: "... *Forgetting those things which are behind, and reaching forth unto those things which are before, I press toward the mark for the prize of the high calling of God in Christ Jesus.*"

If we learn the secret of totally trusting in the Lord, He will lead us on a path that we never thought possible. Even if we've taken some detours from His original path,

He will help us find peace, contentment, and blessing all along the way—and bring us through to our divine destination with joy!

CHAPTER 14

FOR SUCH A TIME AS THIS

You may have started out many years ago on an exciting mission for the Lord, but somehow you were distracted from the path. You may have even lost sight of the call. Or perhaps you've gotten so far off course that you thought, *God, I'll never find my way back.*

But the Lord is saying to you today, "I came off the main road to find you, and I'm picking you up this very moment and putting you back on your course in life."

My friend, now is not the time to draw back. Now is the time for each one of us to take our place in the Kingdom of God.

I believe the time is short. The coming of the Lord is near. There's a lost and dying world out there that needs a Savior. Our mission is to go to them and win them to the Lord.

If we want to accomplish our mission, we're going to have to stir ourselves up. We're going to have to keep that newness and freshness of our faith. We cannot grow stale in serving the Lord, and we cannot forget our purpose—to be witnesses for the Lord Jesus Christ.

God has been keeping many of us on the back burner for such a time as this. But the fire of the Holy Ghost is about to permeate our lives as never before, and the lost are going to come into the kingdom in droves.

This is an exciting time to be alive! I believe great things are about to happen. We have a big mission to accomplish—a big assignment from the Lord.

A Young Girl Saves Her People

Esther was a young Jewish woman in the Bible who had a big mission to accomplish for God. If you recall the story, Esther had been chosen to be the queen of Persia. A man named Haman convinced the king to sign a decree that would cause all the Jews in the land to be executed (see Esther chapters 3–8). But the king didn't know that his queen was also a Jew.

Esther's uncle Mordecai became so distraught over the situation that he appealed to Esther for help. He told her, "You've got to go before the king and plead the case for our people."

But Esther reminded him that if anyone went before the king when he hadn't called for that person, the penalty was death. The only way that person's life would be spared was if the king held out his golden scepter. In other words, if Esther went to the king when he hadn't called for her, she was risking her life.

Mordecai responded, "If this decree is carried out, your life isn't going to be spared either." Then he added, ". . . *Yet who knows whether you have come to the kingdom for such a time as this?"* (Esther 4:14 NKJV).

Did you know that God is looking down from His throne in Heaven right now and saying to you, just as He said to Esther, "You were born for such a time as this"? You have a purpose, a destiny, and a calling. Jeremiah 29:11 says, *"'For I know the plans I have for you,' declares the Lord, 'plans to prosper you and not to harm you, plans to give you hope and a future'"* (NIV). Never ever doubt that God has a good plan for your life!

What if Esther Had Gone to the King at the Wrong Time?

Esther told Mordecai to ask the Jews in that city to fast and pray for three days before she went to see the king. On the third day, she put on her royal robes and went into the inner court of the king's palace. When the king saw her, he held out his golden scepter to her and offered to grant any request she might have—up to half of his kingdom!

The king was furious when he found out that Haman had tricked him into signing a decree to destroy the Jews. So he ordered Haman to be put to death on the same gallows he had built to hang Esther's uncle Mordecai. Suddenly, Esther—a young Jewish girl—became the savior of her people.

There was a reason why this young woman was chosen to become the queen of Persia. God strategically placed her in that position "for such a time as this." He ordered her footsteps so she would be in the right place at the right time to save her people from destruction.

Let's think about that for just a moment. What if Esther had gone to the king at the wrong time? She might have failed in her mission and she might have even lost her life! The timing of God's plan is more important than we can possibly imagine.

It was absolutely necessary for Esther to go before the king at just the right moment, and it's necessary for us to move at the right time too. That's why it's so important for us to be sensitive to the Holy Spirit. We need to follow the steps God has for our lives—*every* step of the way.

'You're Changed People'

Ken and I had a very dramatic experience a few years ago that illustrates how God prepared us "for such a time as this." Just before my father-in-law passed away, Ken received an urgent phone call from his dad, saying that he wasn't able to go to a meeting he had scheduled in Las Vegas. So he asked us to go and take his place.

As soon as my husband gave me the news, I began to panic. I thought, *Oh my goodness, this meeting is only three days away! Dear Lord, what am I going to do?*

So I cried out to my Heavenly Father, "God, I'm not prepared. I don't have my 1,500 pages of notes that my husband always teases me about." (Ken says that he could preach for a whole year from the notes I have for one sermon!)

Then the Lord said something powerful to me. He said, "Lynette, I've been preparing you for this moment for 16 years." In other words, He was telling me, "I have prepared you for such a time as this."

When I heard those words, peace began to flood my heart. I grabbed my fragments of notes that I had used over the years and said, "Okay, God, I've got my four notebooks with two or three pages of notes, and I'm depending on You to help me get them together."

When Ken and I went to Las Vegas for that meeting, my husband preached the evening services and I ministered during the morning services. Yes, there were times when my stomach was tied in knots. There were times when I was upset because I knew the people came expecting to hear Brother Hagin speak, and it was me—a woman—not a man. But I kept trusting the Lord, and we had a wonderful time, a glorious time, at those meetings!

I'll never forget a particular man who came up to me after one of the services and said, "I'll be honest with you. I was quite disappointed when I came to these meetings and saw that Brother Hagin wasn't here. I really wanted to hear Brother Hagin speak. On top of that, you're a woman and I thought, *What can I learn from you?*"

All the time he was talking, I just kept on smiling. If there's one thing I've learned to do in the ministry, it's to smile—no matter what!

Then he continued, "But I've been so blessed by listening to you. The revelation you've taught us about prayer is wonderful, and I'm so excited now about praying!" That experience just showed me that if you will do what God has called you to do and keep on smiling, the Lord will come through for you.

After Brother Hagin went home to be with the Lord, Ken and I had to fulfill all of his speaking obligations. Our hearts were heavy because of the loss we had suffered. But as we endeavored to comfort the people who came to those meetings, God showed himself mightily.

The anointing on us was so strong that several of the ministers who attended those crusade services told us, "When you touched us as you prayed, it felt like a bolt of lightning!" Then they added, "You are changed people. It seems as if you changed overnight."

I just looked at them and smiled. "No, we didn't change overnight," I replied. "God has been preparing us for this day for many years."

And you haven't changed overnight either. God has been preparing you and positioning you for many years for such a time as this. That yearning you've felt down on the inside was put there by the Lord, and it's been growing stronger and stronger—a yearning to fulfill His call. And yet you've been thinking, "I have too many battle scars. The Enemy has zapped me too many times. I'll never make it."

But God is saying to you, "Your scars are healed. I've set you free. You're ready to fulfill My plan."

Like Esther, you've been created and prepared by the Lord for a special mission, a special purpose. He's ordered your footsteps. You're here by divine providence, prepared and positioned for such a time as this!

Are you willing to commit to the purpose? To the calling? To the assignment God has for you? Just as Esther committed her way to the Lord, you have to choose to follow His path.

I encourage you to decide in your heart this very moment that you will accomplish what God has created you to do. Determine that you will fulfill your divine destiny. Will you pray this prayer with me and make a fresh commitment to the Lord right now?

Heavenly Father, I thank You that You have created me. You have called me. You have commissioned me and equipped me for such a time as this. I determine in my heart that I will fulfill what You have called me to do.

I will run my race. I will finish my course. I will keep the faith. I will not let anything deter me. I will stay focused. I will maintain my purpose. I will catch the vision You have for my life and never lose sight of it. In Jesus' Name, I pray. Amen.

Remember, God has brought you to this place and positioned you for such a time as this. You're on His launching pad this very moment. Are you ready to fly? You've been walking and you've been running, but now the Holy Spirit is preparing you *to soar* into the things of God!

When you catch a glimpse of the bigness of God's plan, you'll be amazed! You'll marvel at what He has planned for you. In many cases, it won't be anything like you thought it would be. But as you pray, "Have Thine own way, Lord," God will work His will and His pleasure in you and help you fit perfectly into His divine plan.

Sometimes you won't have any earthly idea why the Lord has taken you along a certain path. But you can rest assured that He is preparing you and positioning you to be in the right place at the right time. And when we all get to Heaven, we'll see the grand and glorious picture that all of our lives together have made! When that day comes, our Lord and Savior will say to us the words that we all want to hear: "Well done, good and faithful servant! You've accomplished what I called you to do. Now enter into the joy of your Lord!"

Why should you consider attending
RHEMA
Bible Training Center?

Here are a few good reasons:

- Training at one of the top Spirit-filled Bible schools anywhere
- Teaching based on steadfast faith in God's Word
- Growth in your spiritual walk coupled with practical training in effective ministry
- Specialization in the area of your choosing:
  Youth or Children's Ministry, Evangelism, Pastoral Care, Missions, or Supportive Ministry
- Optional intensive third-year programs—School of Worship, School of Pastoral Ministry, School of World Missions, and General Extended Studies
- Worldwide ministry opportunities—while you're in school
- An established network of churches and ministries around the world who depend on RHEMA to supply full-time staff and support ministers

Call today for information or application material.
1-888-28-FAITH (1-888-283-2484)
www.rbtc.org

RHEMA Bible Training Center admits students of any race, color, or ethnic origin.

OFFER CODE—BKORD:PRMDRBTC

Word Partner Club:

WORKING *together* TO REACH THE WORLD!

WPC

People. Power. Purpose.

Have you ever dropped a stone into water? Small waves rise up at the point of impact and travel in all directions. It's called a ripple effect. That's the kind of impact Christians are meant to have in this world—the kind of impact that the RHEMA family is producing in the earth today.

The *Word Partner Club* links Christians with a shared interest in reaching people with the Gospel and the message of faith in God.

Together we are reaching across generations, cultures, and nations to spread the Good News of Jesus Christ to every corner of the earth.

To join us in reaching the world, visit **www.rhema.org/wpc** or call, 1-800-54-FAITH (543-2484)